American Bulldog

By Abe Fishman

Paulette Braun, T.J. Calhoun, Alan and Sandy Carey,Carolina Biological Supply, Wil de Veer, Isabelle Français, Bill Jonas, Dr. Dennis Kunkel, Nancy Liguori, Tam C. Nguyen, Phototake, Jean Claude Revy and Nikki Sussman.

Illustrations by Renée Low and Patricia Peters.

The publisher wishes to thank all of the owners of the dogs featured in this book.

Original Print ISBN 978-1-59378-205-4

2030 Main Street, Suite 1400
Irvine, CA 92614
www.facebook.com/luminamediabooks
www.luminamedia.com

My American Bulldog

PUT YOUR PUPPY'S FIRST PICTURE HERE

Dog's Name ____

Date ________________ Photographer ______________________________

Head: Rectangular when viewed from the side.

Skull: Flat and widest between the ears.

Eyes: Round to almond shaped, any color except blue.

Nose: Wide open nostrils, black.

Neck: Muscular, slightly arched.

Muzzle: Square, wide and deep.

Jaws: Should display great strength.

Bite: Scissors to one-quarter-inch undershot.

Shoulders: Very muscular, side sloping shoulder blades.

Chest: Deep brisket, wide but not too wide.

Height: 19 to 27 inches.

Physical Characteristics of the American Bulldog

(from the National American Bulldog Association Standard)

Contents

The American Bulldog's ancestry can be traced to purely American origins; the breed evolved from other breeds in the United States.

History of the

AMERICAN BULLDOG

THE ORIGIN OF THE AMERICAN BULLDOG IN ITS HOMELAND

As we begin this chapter, it is important for you to fully understand how completely misunderstood this breed is in the US and throughout the rest of the world. You will be presented with the history of the American Bulldog breed here, and this history may differ from written histories you will come across elsewhere. If you would rather simplify matters and believe one formal "history," then believe this one. If you find yourself becoming a real student of the breed, however, read them all and, when you have done that, ask yourself which written history makes the most sense. After all, any theory presented should be tested, and I certainly encourage you to test mine.

In the United States, where the American Bulldog breed originated, many believe that the American Bulldog is a breed of British origin, brought to the United States by the ancestors of early settlers from England. The

American Bulldogs are mostly white, often with striking patches of color.

FROM HUTCHINSON'S POPULAR AND ILLUSTRATED DOG ENCYCLOPAEDIA.

Ch. Impresario, in 1903, was the leading pillar of the English Bulldog breed. He does not look very much like the modern American Bulldog.

claim is that the American Bulldog is of pure English Bulldog stock and it exists today in the form in which it was brought to the United States centuries ago. Proponents of this theory totally ignore the fact that at the time the American Bulldog first appeared in the United States, no dog even remotely similar to this breed existed anywhere else in the world, or had ever existed anywhere else in the world, including in England. The theory

The English Bulldog, which has incorrectly been reputed to be the ancestor of the American Bulldog. Although one may assume that the two breeds share a common heritage, the author's theory refutes a similar ancestry.

SOMEBODY TO BLAME

House-training a puppy can be frustrating for the puppy and the owner alike. The puppy does not instinctively understand the difference between defecating on the pavement outside and on the ceramic tile in the kitchen. He is confused and frightened by his human's exuberant reactions to his natural urges. The owner, arguably the more intelligent of the duo, is also frustrated that he cannot convince his puppy to obey his commands and instructions.

In frustration, the owner may struggle with the temptation to discipline the puppy, scold him or even strike him on the rear end. These harsh corrections are unnecessary and inappropriate, serving to defeat your purpose in gaining your puppy's trust and respect. Don't blame your nine-week-old puppy. Blame yourself for not being 100% consistent in the puppy's lessons and routine. The lesson here is simple: try harder and your puppy will succeed.

put the pup into his den. If he's new to a crate, toss in a small biscuit for him to chase the first few times. At night, after he's been outside, he should sleep in his crate. The crate may be kept in his designated area at night or, if you want to be sure to hear those wake-up yips in the morning, put the crate in a corner of your bedroom. However, don't make any response whatsoever to whining or crying. If he's completely ignored, he'll settle down and get to sleep.

Good bedding for a young puppy is an old folded bath towel or an old blanket, something that is easily washable and disposable if necessary ("accidents" will happen!). Never put newspaper in the puppy's crate. Also, those old ideas about adding a clock to replace his mother's heartbeat, or a hot-water bottle to replace her warmth, are just that—old ideas. The clock could drive the puppy nuts, and the hot-water bottle could end up as a very soggy waterbed! An extremely good breeder would have introduced your puppy to the crate by letting two pups sleep together for a couple of nights, followed by several nights alone. How thankful you will be if you found that breeder!

Safe toys in the pup's crate or area will keep him occupied, but monitor their condition closely. Discard any toys that show signs of being chewed to bits. Squeaky parts, bits of stuffing or plastic or any other small pieces can cause intestinal blockage or possibly choking if swallowed.

Progressing with Potty-Training

After you've taken your puppy out and he has relieved himself in the area you've selected, he

The Staffordshire Bull Terrier, shown here, was originally brought to America as a fighting dog. The American Pit Bull Terrier derived from this breed.

important that you research what I just told you. In order to test my theory, you will need to find pictures of early American Bulldogs and compare the dogs in those early pictures with known English Bulldogs of that time or earlier. Remember that this is an old breed and when I say that you will need to find early pictures, I don't mean pictures from 1980. I mean pictures known to date to 1940 or earlier. You must realize that American Bulldogs of 1980 or thereabout were already being crossed to other breeds, including the Bullmastiff and English Bulldog, not to enhance the breed's working ability but rather to make the pups more marketable to novice puppy purchasers. These puppy purchasers were not in the market for an authentic American Bulldog, but instead they were in search of a pet they could relate to as a "Bulldog."

At this point, let's assume that we know what the American Bulldog is *not*, as a result of having read what has already been said. The question remains as to what the American Bulldog *is*. If the American Bulldog is of purely American origin, it had to come from somewhere, and the question remains as to where the American Bulldog did come from. If the breed evolved in the United States, from what breed or breeds did it evolve? To get to the bottom of this question, we will need to know a little about two closely related breeds.

One breed that is very similar to the American Bulldog and that

CANIS LUPUS

"Grandma, what big teeth you have!" The gray wolf, a familiar figure in fairy tales and legends, has had its reputation tarnished and its population pummeled over the centuries. Yet it is the descendants of this much-feared creature to which we open our homes and hearts. Our beloved dog, *Canis domesticus*, derives directly from the gray wolf, a highly social canine that lives in elaborately structured packs. In the wild, the gray wolf can range from 60 to 175 pounds, standing between 25 and 40 inches in height.

is also known to have evolved in the United States is the American Pit Bull Terrier. The American Pit Bull Terrier, more commonly known as the "Pit Bull," is essentially the American expression of the English Staffordshire Bull Terrier. As immigrants from England and Ireland began to make America their home, some brought their little "Staffords" along with them. One of the primary uses for the Staffords brought to the United States was fighting in organized "game-dog"

The American Bulldog had to be larger than the Staffords in order to protect the herd and perform his other duties effectively.

The breed's strength and impressive build are evident even in American Bulldog youngsters.

There is quite a range of height and weight in the American Bulldog breed. This dog is on the heavier, bulkier side.

matches. Such game-dog matches involved the pitting of one fighting dog against another of the same breed, the same sex and the same size. For purposes of these matches, it didn't make any difference what size the dogs involved were, as long as both dogs were of the same size. With Staffords, the dogs involved were small (in the 35-pound range).

Once in the United States, however, a few influences became responsible for the gradual metamorphosis of the game-bred English and Irish Staffordshire dogs into the Pit Bull. One of these factors was simply personal choice and selective breeding. America was the land of plenty, and a dog owner in the US could afford to feed a slightly larger dog than could a coal miner living and working in Staffordshire, England. Additionally, other ideas came to mind about uses fit for such a tough, fast, agile and determined little dog. One of these uses was farm and ranch work.

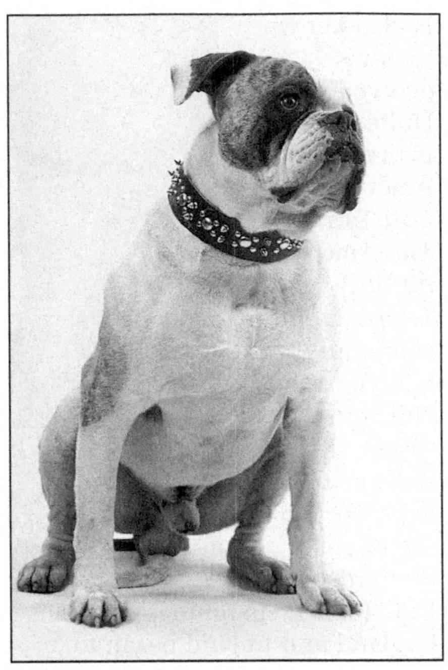

The American Pit Bull Terrier was bred originally to be a fighting and catch dog. Although very strong and agile, it was still a bit smaller than the farmers wanted for catch work.

A dog that was to be used for farm and ranch work had to be larger than the small fighting Staffords were. The reason for this is that among the farm dog's duties was protecting the farmer's livestock from free-running dogs. A dog that spends much of its time running free will often become aggressive toward valuable livestock, and farmers valued a tough dog that had the willingness and ability to attack and run off such "wild" dogs.

Although bred for working ability, not looks, the American Bulldog is quite an attractive breed.

It is possible that the primarily white coat of the American Bulldog originated in the early catch-dog breeds.

Another demand placed upon the farm and ranch dog was what is commonly known in the United States as "catch work." Catch work is the securing and holding of "free-range" livestock that has grown to a size at which it must be brought to slaughter. Imagine the huge expanses of land available for use by early American farmers and ranchers. If a farmer or rancher who had a large parcel of land available to him wanted to raise hogs, for example, the least expensive method of raising the hogs was to "brand" the animals so that everyone would know to whom the hogs belonged, and then allow them to roam free. This worked well until the time came to collect a mature hog.

Once such livestock had spent its early life maturing into a wild animal, it was inclined to run from people and to attack those it could not run from. If a rancher was to catch and tie the free-range livestock, that farmer needed the assistance of a dog that could run down the livestock in question, grab the animal and hold it until the farmer or rancher could tie the livestock. Such work demanded a larger dog than the English Staffordshire Bull Terrier, and the animal that was to become the Pit Bull was developed to be a combination "larger fighting dog" and "catch dog." It is probable that the increased size of the Pit Bull was the result of purely selective breeding as opposed to being the result of Staffords having been crossed to other breeds.

With the aforementioned in mind, imagine now that a farmer or rancher needed a catch dog and that the farmer or rancher had absolutely no interest in fighting dogs. Instead, he wanted a somewhat larger dog than the Pit Bull, because the Pit Bull, while suitable for use as a catch dog because of the breed's tenacity, strength, agility and speed, was still rather small for the work at hand. What the farmer wanted was a Pit Bull in the 65- to 85-pound range, but at the time no such dog was known. These farmers indeed had "catch breeds" of their own and had been using these dogs for catch work for generations. Some of these hard-working catch breeds still exist in small numbers in rural areas of the United States. One fine example of a working catch breed is the Yellow Black Mouth Cur, made famous by the Disney movie *Old Yeller.* Another native American working catch breed is the Louisiana Catahoula Leopard Dog, so called because it is native to the state of Louisiana, specifically the Catahoula Lake parishes of Louisiana, and because it is a spotted breed.

Both the Cur dog and the "Cat" are larger dogs than the Pit Bull. If farmers and ranchers of old were interested in a working catch dog, it would have made no difference to them if their catch dog stock was pure Catahoula, pure Cur or mixed-bred Pit Bull. What was important was that, in the end, the catch dogs were hard, determined, agile, strong and large

CARE AND TRAINING

The behavior and personality of your American Bulldog will reflect your care and training more than any breed characteristics or indications. Remember that these dogs require a purposeful existence, and plan your relationship around activities that serve this most basic and important need. All the good potential of the breed will necessarily follow.

enough to catch a mature hog, yet small enough to maneuver about without getting injured or harmed by the livestock. A combination of Pit Bull and these larger indigenous catch dogs could have produced such a versatile working dog. This author believes that it is highly likely that such early crossbreeding produced the breed we now know as the American Bulldog.

A question arises when we ask why American Bulldogs are so commonly pure white in color. One possibility is that many old Staffords and later many Pit Bulls of old were white. These white pit dogs were used in early catch-dog breeding. Another possibility is that one of the early catch breeds used in the crosses was either all white or at least frequently seen in white. We do see that many Catahoula Leopard Dogs carry genes for white coat coloring, and it is possible that this is part of the reason that American Bulldogs were and still are white. It is interesting to note here that many Catahoulas have blue, or even "clear" or "glass" eyes. This is a rather "spooky" genetic anomaly common to Catahoulas. Similarly, blue eyes occur among American Bulldogs, too.

It is also possible that the white coat of the American Bulldog came from the use of early white Pit Bull genetic stock

The Yellow Black Mouth Cur dog, which Walt Disney made famous in the movie *Old Yeller*. This is a scene from the movie showing the Cur dog and the young actor Tommy Kirk.

Many Catahoulas have striking blue or even glassy clear eyes.

A pair of Catahoula Leopard Dogs. This breed may have featured heavily in the ancestry of the American Bulldog.

in the production of early working cross-bred catch dogs. If so, the white coat of the American Bulldog might well account for the white coloring we often see in the coat of the Catahoula Leopard Dog. We may never know for sure. In looking for evidence that such crosses were of interest to rural American agriculturists, however, we can point to similar crosses that are still being conducted today. One such cross is the Plott Hound (an American breed similar to the Catahoula) to the Pit Bull. The Plott-Hound-to-Pit-Bull cross is often conducted to produce a bear-hunting dog. It is known to produce a dog with the courage and tenacity to track and get in close to a bear, causing the dog to "tree" or "bay." These dogs are also known to be smart enough to stay a safe distance from the bear to avoid getting themselves killed. Interestingly, the Catahoula is also known to be an effective bear dog for the same reasons and, in fact, in days gone by, the breed was referred to by some as the Catahoula Bear Dog.

In any event, it is highly likely that the American Bulldog originated in rural America as a ranch and farm dog used for catch work and for protecting livestock from marauding packs of wild dogs. If so, it is likely that the kinds of crosses just described are the crosses that gave rise to the American Bulldog. Ideally, then, the American Bulldog would have been a hard, fast, working, tenacious, medium- to large-sized dog (65 to 85 pounds). From early photographs, we know that these dogs were always white. We also know that in order to be most effective at the task of catching wild free-range livestock, the level or scissors bite would have been preferable to the undershot bite. As expected, early photographs depict American Bulldogs with working scissors bites.

SEMENCIC'S THEORY

It should be noted that the theory of the breed's history presented here was first developed and put forth by the American breed historian Dr. Carl Semencic. Semencic can also be credited with having popularized this breed at a time when it had become almost extinct in the United States and before it had been introduced to other parts of the world. It is the author's opinion that Semencic's theory makes more sense than any other being put forth, and it is offered here as the true history of the American Bulldog breed.

THE MORE RECENT HISTORY OF THE AMERICAN BULLDOG

Readers who recognize the modern American Bulldog will undoubtedly have questions about the breed's ancestry as set forth in this book. After all, the breed described is a smaller, more agile

The Plott Hound, shown here, is often crossed with Pit Bulls to produce a bear-hunting dog. Pure-bred Plotts are very able hunters in their own right.

BACK FROM THE BRINK

In 1980, the American Bulldog breed was at the very door of extinction. You could literally count on one hand the number of breeders producing these dogs for use as working dogs. Every breeder producing American Bulldogs, then known as the American Pit Bulldog (divulging the breed's fighting ancestry), lived in the American Southeast, in the states of Georgia, Alabama and the rest of the Deep South region. It is very likely that had nothing at all happened to popularize the breed, it would not have been long before the American Bulldog would have become extinct.

breed than the dogs we know as American Bulldogs today. The breed described here had a level bite, and many of today's American Bulldogs are undershot. In fact, some of the written breed standards according to which these dogs are being shown and judged today describe vastly oversized, undershot dogs. Some of the dogs being shown are not even white in color. Why should this be the case if this book's theory is true?

In order to understand how the American Bulldog breed evolved from the creature it once was to the creature we see today, we will need to understand the breed's more recent history. When I refer to the breed's recent history, I mean specifically the year 1978 to the present. Before 1978, the American Bulldog was a very homogeneous creature with regard to its genotype and its phenotype. It ranged in size from 60- to 65-pound females to males that reached a maximum of 85 pounds. The vast majority of these dogs were all white, and those that were not all white were mostly white. The bite was level. The overall body shape was much like that of the Pit Bull Terrier, but the breed did not display obvious terrier genetic influence. The tail of the breed tended to be thicker and more "feathered" than that of the Pit Bull.

The very late 1970s to about

POPULARITY PROS AND CONS

The good news is that as a result of Dr. Carl Semencic's writing about the breed, the American Bulldog was brought to the attention of American pure-bred fanciers nationwide. The bad news is that it was not long after the American pure-bred and rare-breed fanciers became aware of the breed that a demand for oversized Bulldogs was created by these novice breed fanciers. Many American Bulldog breeders, having never witnessed any demand for their dogs before, were more than happy to cross their Bulldogs with other breeds in order to create whatever dog it was that prospective puppy buyers wanted. After all, those who were calling for pups at this time were not asking for dogs that could actually work the ranch or the farm. They were asking for pups that would grow into dogs that would simply look the part of the "big tough Bulldog." It was at this time that the bastardization of the American Bulldog breed began.

1980 found the breed low in popularity. Few breeders had any interest in the American Bulldog. Only farmers and ranchers owned the breed at this time. The breed was completely unknown to the dog fancy at large. No articles had ever been written anywhere in the world about the breed and the only information in print at all were a few advertisements that appeared in a farmer's (stockman's) pulp paper journal published in a small Texas town. These advertised American Bulldogs were bred by farmers solely for sale to other farmers. They were cheap to buy and not really thought of as pure-bred dogs at all. They were strictly working dogs.

There were many reasons for the fall in the American Bulldog's popularity. It was not as if these dogs had a long way to go in order to reach a condition of total non-existence. They had always been rare and they were rapidly becoming totally obscure. Even more significant was the fact that the Pit Bull breed exploded in

The American Bulldog was not bred to be a guard dog, but his looks alone are usually enough to scare off a potential intruder.

A European-bred American Bulldog with very nice conformation. The popularity of the breed in the US made its way across the Atlantic.

popularity throughout the US in the early 1980s. Not only did the Pit Bull suddenly become popular but the influx of novices getting involved with the Pit Bull created a great demand for larger Pit Bulls. Whereas once the American Bulldog was seen as being a Pit Bull-like dog, only larger, suddenly it was the same size as a larger Pit Bull (only not as hard and without the great fighting reputation). This gave rise to a situation in which general dog fanciers had no reason to become interested in American Bulldogs, and even stock-dog and working-dog men found the larger Pit Bull to be easier to come by and perfectly satisfactory for farm and ranch work.

Fortunately for the American Bulldog, the breed captured the interest of American pure-bred dog historian Dr. Carl Semencic. Semencic had begun to research the breed during the late 1970s, and, by the very early 1980s, he had begun to publish articles about it. He wrote the first article about the breed in the American show-dog magazine *Dog World.* He titled the article "Introducing the American Bulldog" and offered an in-depth review of the breed and its condition. In 1984, he authored the popular book *The World of Fighting Dogs*, which included the first chapter ever written about the American Bulldog breed.

MODERN LINES OF AMERICAN BULLDOGS

When the American rare-breed fancy discovered the American Bulldog in about 1982, there were three breeders who were best known for their involvement in the breed. Today we think of

This dog possesses many typical breed characteristics: mostly white, black nose and impressive head.

primarily two but sometimes all three of them as being the fathers of distinct "lines" of modern American Bulldogs. One of these men was Joe Painter of Chicago, Illinois. Painter was widely thought to have been interested in breeding primarily fighting dogs, and his American Bulldogs were generally thought to have been crosses between American Bulldogs and highly game-bred American Pit Bull Terriers from the Chicago area.

America in the 1980s saw the development of several distinct lines of American Bulldogs that greatly influenced the dogs we see today.

The second of these men was Alan Scott of Alabama. Scott was a young man in 1982 and could not have been involved in Bulldogs for very long. At the time, the American Bulldogs he owned and produced were pure working-type Bulldogs of the type that had been around for many decades. Scott turned his interests away from American Bulldog breeding for a few years, and it was only during the mid-1990s that he returned to it, using the stock that was available to him then.

This dog's undershot jaw is typical of many American Bulldogs today but would not have been functional for the early working catch dogs.

The third of these men was one John D. Johnson of the state of Georgia. Johnson's Bulldogs had been essentially the same as Scott's prior to the late 1970s. More than any other breeder then or since, Johnson responded to the novice puppy purchasers' demands for oversized, "bully-looking" dogs. Seemingly overnight, "Johnson dogs" grew dramatically in size. Whereas in 1980 and before, Johnson's big dogs weighed no more than 80 or

Although the "lines" of American Bulldog are relatively new, this is by no means a new breed.

85 pounds, by 1985 Johnson was advertising Bulldogs that weighed as much as 135 pounds. The appearance of the dogs changed just as dramatically.

There are many rumors about the many breeds with which Johnson crossed his Bulldogs in order to achieve the size and the entirely new look. Rather than speculate here, let us pass on the following information. At the core of Johnson's bloodlines from about 1980 on is a bitch by the name of Bullmede's Queen. Queen was bred and owned by Mr. Dave Leavitt, then of Spring Grove, Pennsylvania. Leavitt was very honest about the breeding techniques he used in his own production of dogs; he intended to recreate the "Olde English Bulldogge," theoretically the Bulldog in its original form. An examination of Leavitt's bloodlines will clearly demonstrate that Queen, an important bitch in Johnson's breeding of American Bulldogs, was in fact part Pit Bull, part show-variety English Bulldog and part Bullmastiff. The reader can speculate along with so many others regarding what else Johnson may have crossed into his "American Bulldog" lines from that point on. What we do know for sure is that his dogs became so different from all other American Bulldogs that many no longer consider his dogs to be of the same breed.

We must understand this if we are to find a proper Bulldog for ourselves and to attempt to preserve the true American

THE OLD AND THE NEW

The three lines mentioned here, and all other lines you will hear reference to, are newly created lines, but the American Bulldog is by no means a newly created breed. This is a very old working breed that has been very adversely impacted by cross-breeding in recent years. This breed was essentially pure-bred before any of the men whose names are connected to the various lines were born. It remained in a very homogeneous form for many decades, and it was only when we began to think in terms of "lines" that the breed became as thoroughly genetically diluted as it is today.

Bulldog for dog owners in years to come. It is not an American Bulldog out of any one of these lines, or an American Bulldog out of a conglomeration of these lines, that will be the best American Bulldog. It is a Bulldog of old working lines that will be the true American Bulldog.

THE AMERICAN BULLDOG IN EUROPE

During the 1990s, the explosion of interest in the American Bulldog began to spread beyond the shores of the United States. With all of the cross-breeding that has occurred and continues to occur among American Bulldog breeders in the US, it is highly beneficial to the breed to find itself in the hands of European breeders. Hopefully, European breeders will not view cross-breeding to other breeds as an option when breeding to improve their American Bulldog stock. Also, European breeders have quickly expressed an interest in breeding dogs with a willingness to work, rather than dogs intended only to scare their neighbors. One word of caution: keep in mind that protection work was never the primary function of the American Bulldog. Catch work and ranch work is what this breed was designed for. While testing a dog in Schutzhund trials demonstrates a certain degree of working ability within this breed, one must bear in mind

PERSONAL PROTECTOR

Many of today's American Bulldogs are purchased for basic home guardian and personal protection work. One thing the various lines of American Bulldogs have in common is the fact that all tend to be useful protection dogs, since breeders tend to favor stock with strong protective instincts. Further, owners of American Bulldogs often engage in training their dogs to become guard dogs. What owners need to realize, though, is that this is not the breed's original function and that proper protection is obtained only through proper training. Furthermore, the American Bulldog's wonderful pet potential should never be overlooked.

THE FAMILY PET

Many an American Bulldog is brought home to be a family pet, too. The Bulldog often makes a fine family pet. It is not an overly active breed. It is not a breed that is likely to roam away from its home property. It can be, and often is, a playful breed, and while any play between any dog and any child should always be supervised by an adult, the American Bulldog is usually a good pet for an older child. Pet American Bulldog owners often attest to their dogs' loving and even goofy personalities.

that the American Bulldog was never intended to be a man-biter. This breed was developed to be tested on game much more deadly than man, and the extraordinary agility and tenacity demonstrated while catching free-range hogs in the field are infinitely more dangerous and demanding than "man work" will ever be.

MODERN USES FOR THE AMERICAN BULLDOG

As we know, the American Bulldog was very likely developed for use as a farm dog. The responsibilities of a farm dog were varied. They included catch work (catching and holding mature livestock for slaughter) and the protection of livestock from free-roaming dogs and packs of wild dogs. The American Bulldog in its working form is still used for this kind of work today. Given the popularity of the breed among pet owners presently, the percentage of American Bulldogs actually employed for farm and catch work is quite small indeed.

We have alluded to the fact that some American Bulldogs, such as those of the "Painter Line," were used as fighting dogs in the past. It was not only the modern cross-bred American Bulldog that was used as a fighting dog, however. There are many old-time stories from people who knew the American Bulldog breed during the 1940s and 1950s that tell of serious organized dog fights in which American Bulldogs, rather than Pit Bulls, were matched.

The bottom line is that today's American Bulldog has much to offer a family who will raise him right, devote time and effort to train and socialize him properly and give him the attention he needs. This breed is a wonderful companion, but the American Bulldog must know who's the boss—you!

Characteristics of the

AMERICAN BULLDOG

In discussing the temperament of the American Bulldog, we must consider that the range in type within the breed today is so great and the genetic material composing this breed is so varied that the physical and temperamental characteristics of your dog will depend upon his specific ancestry. One or more of the giant breeds were crossed into some American Bulldog lines in the recent past, so common sense dictates that the lines in question will produce dogs displaying the characteristics of those giant breeds. On the other end of the spectrum, if the Pit Bull was crossed into the line from which your dog descends, chances are that your dog will display characteristics that are more like the Pit Bull. If your dog is from pure, or nearly pure, old-time working American Bulldog lines, that is another matter altogether.

An American Bulldog with another breed known for an impressive-looking head and strength—the Dogue de Bordeaux.

SUSPICIOUS MINDS

The American Bulldog is a protective dog, but he should never be an overly hot-headed dog. He should greet strangers with only mild suspicion, when these strangers are in the company of the dog's master. An American Bulldog should never appear threatening to any friend who has come to the home. When called upon to defend, however, he should do so with authority and be prepared to die in defense of his human family.

If we are going to strive to preserve the pure American Bulldog, however, it is also important that we understand the character that defines it. Any breed displays both a typical look and a typical character, and it is a combination of the two that should be selected in the show ring and for any breeding program. With this in mind, let's take a look at the desirable character of the true American Bulldog.

While we've emphasized the American Bulldog's working ability, we should also mention that he has a silly side and likes to goof off with friends.

The true American Bulldog is among the most reliable working dogs ever developed. Remember the job that the working American Bulldog was produced to do. It was essentially a "catch dog," sent out to attack, grab and hold highly dangerous free-range livestock, such as the Arkansas razorback boar. Once the dog had caught the livestock, the dog's job was to hold that livestock while it was either killed or, more commonly, tied by the dog's owner. Bearing in mind that the razorback boar is such a lethal animal, the rancher's life literally depended upon both the ability and the reliability of his catch dog.

The true American Bulldog is certainly a reliable dog. It is also a steady dog and a loyal dog. The working Bulldog had to have the tenacity to catch and fight for his life while always recognizing that he was part of a team that consisted of the dog and his human companion. This is a dog with both the physical ability and the energy to work hard and quickly, but he is also a dog that knows when to relax and lie quietly by the fire.

The American Bulldog should be a fun-loving dog that enjoys time in the yard and walks with his master. In fact, this is a breed that exudes happiness very clearly, and those who own a good representative of this breed will quickly come to know the meaning of the expression "a Bulldog

MALE OR FEMALE?

An important consideration is the sex of your American Bulldog puppy. For a family companion, an American Bulldog bitch is the best choice, considering the female's inbred concern for all young creatures and her accompanying tolerance and patience. Regardless of which sex you choose, a pet male should be neutered and a pet female should be spayed.

smile." In brief, in the breed's true form, this is a dog you will enjoy owning and one you will remember fondly for the rest of your life. It is the quintessential pet, friend and home protector.

HEALTH PROBLEMS SPECIFIC TO THE AMERICAN BULLDOG

As we know, cross-breeding between American Bulldogs and other breeds has been very common since the late 1970s. As such, when we consider the health problems that occur and that occur with a high degree of frequency in this breed, we must consider that depending upon the genetic lines of each particular dog, health considerations may vary. The following are health problems that affect the breed as a whole. Not every health problem listed here will occur in every American Bulldog line, but it is important that your dog's veterinarian realizes that all of these problems exist within the modern genetic stock that defines this breed.

The defects that can occur in the American Bulldog are enlarged hearts, kidney and thyroid disorders, undersized lungs, hip dysplasia, elbow dysplasia, entropion, ectropion, bone cancer, deafness and blindness. Some also can suffer from skin problems like allergies and mange. Needless to say, well-established working stock will produce healthier dogs. Breeders should have their dogs

This pose is just for show, but the American Bulldog is certainly capable of giving his bull-and-terrier friends a lift!

tested and certified by both the Orthopedic Foundation for Animals (OFA) and the Canine Eye Registration Foundation (CERF); ask to see this documentation on your pup's parents.

KEEPING YOUR AMERICAN BULLDOG FIT

If this were a book about the Staffordshire Bull Terrier, an appropriate exercise program for your dog would be an easy one to prescribe. Contrarily, if this were a book about the Mastiff or the St. Bernard, a different kind of exercise program would also be easy to recommend. But we aren't talking about Staffordshire Bull Terriers or Mastiffs or St. Bernards or Greyhounds or any other breed here. We are talking about the American Bulldog. The range in type we will see in the two standards, to be discussed later, and in my description of this breed in its proper form make outlining a healthy exercise program for the average dog of this breed impossible.

This does not mean that adequate exercise will not benefit your American Bulldog, however. Exercise certainly will benefit your American Bulldog, and a program of regular exercise should definitely be implemented by the time the dog is nine months old. This simply means that due to the variation of physical type within this breed, brought on by cross-breeding to other breeds of very different types in recent years, you will have to evaluate your dog's type before a program of exercise is implemented. After all, the kind of exercise program that will benefit a fully grown, 85-pound, hard-working stock dog could very well kill a 130-pound dog of the Johnson line, for example.

American Bulldogs are very agile. How many other dogs can jump this high?

Again, the extreme range in type between the stock dog, the later Scott-line dogs, the old Painter-line dogs and the Johnson-line dogs is too great to view one form of exercise as being "right" for the breed. As such, it would be irresponsible of me to recommend a single exercise program as being adequate for all American Bulldogs. With this breed, you will have to evaluate the individual dog you want to keep fit and devise a program based upon what you know your dog to be. An exercise program for an adult dog may be as simple as a regular three-mile walk, three or four times a week on cool days. For working stock dogs, the program may be more strenuous, possibly including outdoor running or even weight pulling.

OWNER CONSIDERATIONS

The American Bulldog is a handsome and athletic companion dog. There is no doubt that this is a pure-bred dog that will continue to attract many admirers. Nonetheless, the American Bulldog is a breed that requires a special kind of owner. One of the most striking attributes of the American Bulldog is his agility. For a dog this size, no dog can compare to the American Bulldog for agility. Such athleticism and energy calls for an owner who has plenty of time to spend with his dog, training, conditioning and just horsing around. The owner himself must be fit and active to keep up with his American Bulldog. This is not to say that the breed doesn't enjoy quiet time, but exercise is a must to keep this fellow trim, fit and mentally and physically balanced. If you are looking for a dog to sleep all day and get all of his exercise indoors or ambling about the yard, this is the wrong breed for you.

Generally speaking, the American Bulldog can be taught fairly easily. This Bulldog is not as stubborn as his Union Jack-clad counterpart. The American Bulldog enjoys spending time with his owner, so training time is a favorite time for this dog. New owners must comprehend that acquiring a dog is tantamount to settling down with a partner. The American Bulldog can live to be well over ten years of age. New owners must be able to predict that their lifestyle over the coming decade can accommodate an American Bulldog.

Fortunately, this breed is among the most versatile dogs in the world. As long as he's by your side, this breed is equally content on a multi-acre estate as he is in an apartment. Provided that the owner is available to offer the dog exercise and attention, the American Bulldog will welcome any comfortable, loving household.

An American Bulldog can be a great friend to children who know how to treat a dog properly. Introductions and interactions should always be supervised.

An ideal situation, however, would be a home with a fenced yard in which the dog can stretch his legs. While it is unlike the American Bulldog to want to wander away from home, a fence is still a must for his safety. Also, since some American Bulldogs can be aggressive with other dogs, it's best to prevent problems by fencing in the yard. The neighborhood cats will also appreciate that your dog can't roam free!

Since the American Bulldog will grow into a protective, dominant guardian, it's important for the owner to be aware of the challenges of puppyhood.

Adolescence promises that your Bulldog will begin to show his dominant instincts. Never permit a puppy to "bully" you about, since this sets a very dangerous precedent as the dog matures. Aggression toward people can never be tolerated, so be ready to show your American Bulldog who's boss right from the start. Since some fighting-dog blood may be pulsing through your puppy's veins, be ready to handle the puppy that growls at every other dog. While you can never totally change "the ways of the scorpion," you can channel the pup's instincts into acceptable behavior. Introductions to other dogs must become a part of your puppy's socialization process. Just as you will want to expose the puppy to all kinds of people in a variety of environments, you will want to introduce your Bulldog pup to other pups and adult dogs. Assuring the American Bulldog pup that other dogs are not "the enemy" will pay off grandly in the later months and years. How you raise your puppy determines how he will react to other people, dogs and animals, so make sure to nurture your pup into a wonderful ambassador for the breed.

Although the American Bulldog is not AKC-recognized, other national organizations register and offer conformation showing for the breed.

FITNESS FOR LIFE

Walking is a basic necessity for every dog, whether he's strong and tall like the American Bulldog or petite and delicate like the Toy Poodle. Owners of American Bulldogs can be sure that this breed loves the quality time on the road, and walking and running are ideal ways of conditioning your American Bulldog. Don't encourage running with young puppies, since the breed matures slowly and excessive exercise when their bones and ligaments are growing may cause long-term damage. Once the American Bulldog reaches a year to 18 months old, the owner can concentrate on conditioning the dog. Many owners jog, hike and cycle with their dogs. Some owners even use treadmills and while these devices are often associated with dogfighters, they can also be responsibly used for exercise.

Breed Standard

AMERICAN BULLDOG

VARIATIONS IN BREED STANDARDS

A breed standard, by definition, describes what the "ideal" example of a particular breed looks and acts like. This written description is devised by fanciers of the breed, usually a parent club, and is submitted to the national kennel club for approval. Since there is such confusion in the American Bulldog breed, we will examine how the dissension among breeders has affected the writing of the breed standard. I began this book by saying that the American Bulldog breed is vastly misunderstood. In order to demonstrate just how misunderstood this breed is in its homeland of the United States, I am going to present to you two current breed standards that supposedly describe the same American Bulldog breed. The NABA (National American Bulldog Association) standard is more of a working-dog standard. The other, the UKC (United Kennel Club) standard is more of an "attempt to appease everyone" standard.

Despite variations in the different breed standards, the American Bulldog has an unmistakable look all its own.

A TRUE DESCRIPTION

Should you find yourself suspicious of the fact that the description of the American Bulldog breed the author has provided differs from one standard you've seen or another, simply take note of the fact that each standard differs from the other as well. Trust whichever standard or description provides you with the image of the breed that you can find in photographs that predate 1975. The best standard will be the one that most accurately describes what this breed has always been and not what this breed has been turned into more recently. Also, in reading the two standards on the next few pages, take careful note of fundamental differences between them, such as coat color, bite, size, etc.

Physical Structure of the American Bulldog

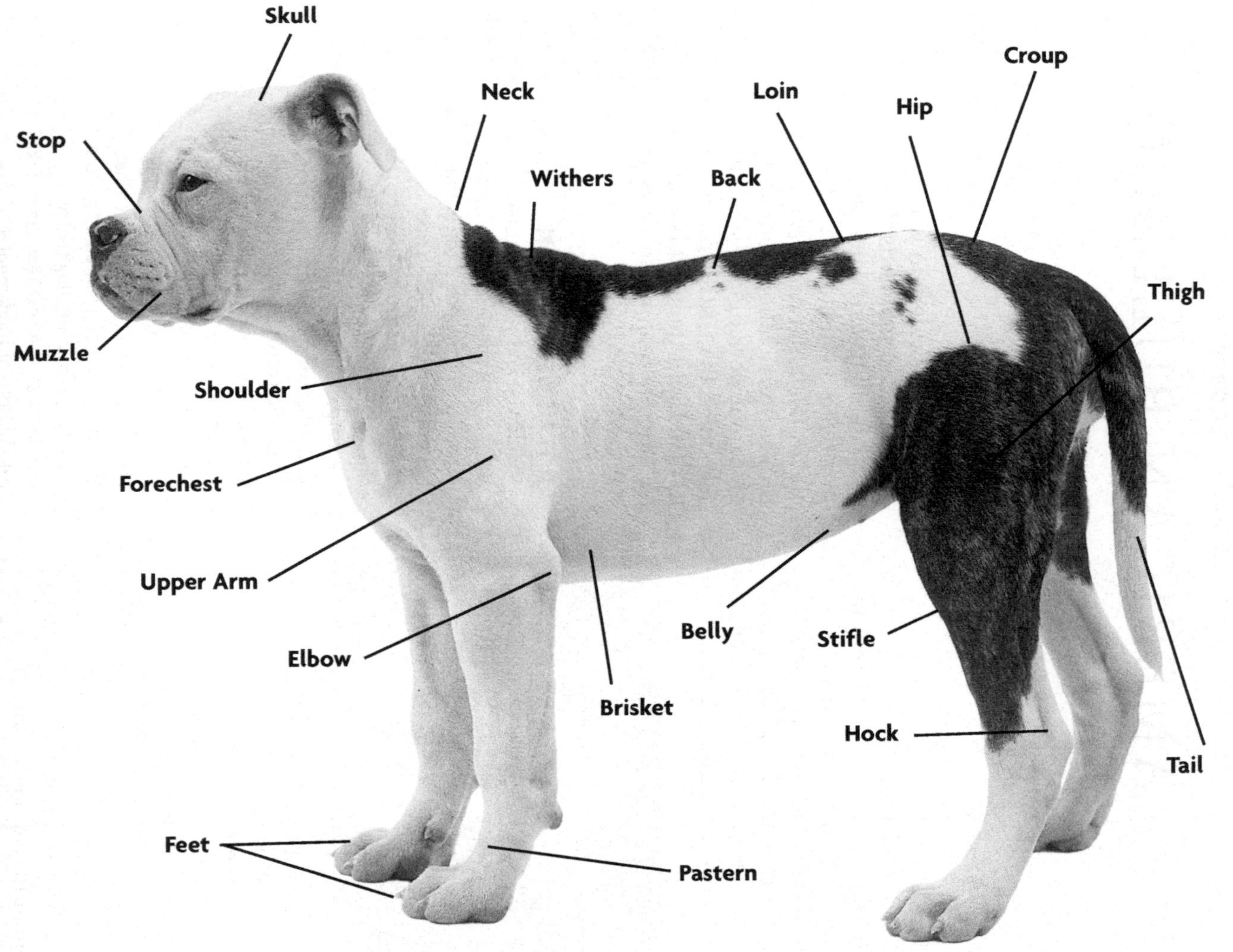

NABA STANDARD FOR THE AMERICAN BULLDOG

Head: Medium length, box-like when viewed from the front. Rectangular when viewed from the side. Skull flat and widest at the ears. Prominent cheeks with little to no wrinkles. Head should be prominent, but not overly so. Should look powerful and quick.

Muzzle: Square, wide and deep. Large jaws, should display great strength. Bite should be scissors to one-quarter-inch undershot. Muzzle should be 35% to 42% of the total length of the head. Should have a noticeable stop at the forehead. Muzzle should be wider at the base and taper slightly to the nose.

Eyes: Round to almond shaped, any color except blue.

Nose: Wide open nostrils, black.

Neck: Muscular, slightly arched. Tapering from shoulder to head.

Shoulders: Very muscular, side sloping shoulder blades.

Back: Medium in length, sloping from rump to withers. Slightly arched at loins, which should be slightly tucked.

Hips: Very muscular, pronounced muscularity.

Stifles: Should be well angled.

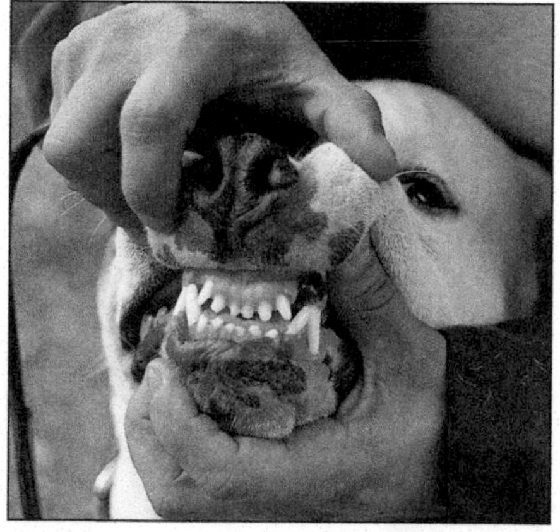

The breed originally had a working scissors bite, although an undershot bite is not uncommon today and even acceptable in breed standards.

Chest: Deep brisket, wide but not too wide.

Coat color: Any color except flat black or any blue.

Weight: Not important as long as structure is sound. Any weight between 85 lb. to 105 lb. for males, 65 lb. to 90 lb. for females.

Height: 19 to 27 inches.

Working dogs will not be penalized for broken teeth, cropped ears or docked tails.

The breed is known for its wide head, conveying a look of power.

UKC STANDARD FOR THE AMERICAN BULLDOG

History

Bulldogs in England were originally working dogs who drove and caught cattle and guarded their masters' property. The breed's strength, courage and familiarity with livestock led to its popularity in the brutal sport of bullbaiting. When this sport was outlawed in England, the original type of Bulldog

An impressive head on a Dutch-bred American Bulldog.

disappeared from Britain and was replaced with the shorter, stockier, less athletic dog we now know as the English Bulldog.

The original Bulldog, however, was preserved by working class immigrants who brought their working dogs with them to the American South. Small farmers and ranchers used this all-around working dog for many tasks. By the end of World War II, however, the breed was almost extinct. Mr. John D. Johnson, a returning war veteran, decided to resurrect this breed. Along with Alan Scott and several other breeders, Johnson began carefully to breed American Bulldogs, keeping careful records and always with an eye for maintaining the breed's health and working abilities.

Because of the many different types of work this breed can do, several distinct lines evolved, each emphasizing the traits needed to do a specific job. The best known lines are usually referred to as the Johnson and Scott types. The Johnson dogs are more massive, with a larger, broader head and shorter muzzle, and a definite undershot bite. The Scott dogs were somewhat lighter in musculature and bone than the Johnson dogs, with a less Mastiff-like head. Today, however, most American Bulldogs have crosses to two or more of these lines and are not as easily distinguishable.

The modern American Bulldog continues to serve as an all-purpose working dog; a fearless and steady guard dog; and a loyal family companion.

The American Bulldog was recognized by the United Kennel Club on January 1, 1999.

General Appearance

The American Bulldog is a powerful, athletic short-coated dog, strongly muscled and well boned. The body is just slightly longer than tall. The head is large and broad with a wide muzzle. Ears are small to medium in size, high set, and may be drop, semi-prick, rose or cropped. The tail may be docked or natural. The American Bulldog comes in solid colors, white with colored patches and brindle. Gender differences are well expressed in this breed, with males typically larger and more muscular than females. Honorable scars resulting from field work are not to be penalized. The American Bulldog should be evaluated as a working dog and exaggerations or faults should be penalized in proportion to how much they interfere with the dog's ability to work.

Characteristics

The essential characteristics of the American Bulldog are those which enable it to work as a hog and cattle catching dog, and a protector of personal property. These tasks require a powerful, agile, confident dog with a large head and powerful jaws. The American Bulldog is a gentle, loving family companion who is fearless enough to face an angry bull or a human intruder. Note: It is common for young American Bulldogs to be somewhat standoffish with strangers and judges should not penalize this. By the time the dog is around 18 months of age, however, the breed's normal confidence asserts itself. *Disqualifications*: Viciousness or extreme shyness; cowardice.

An American Bulldog should appear confident and self-assured, like the Bulldog shown here.

Head

The head is large and broad, giving the impression of great power. When viewed from the side, the skull and muzzle are parallel to one another and joined by a well-defined stop. The stop is very deep and abrupt, almost at a right angle with the muzzle. Despite the depth of the stop, the forehead is wider than it is high.

The broad head, relatively short muzzle, muscular cheeks and large jaws contribute to the overall expression so distinct in the breed.

Skull: The skull is large, flat, deep and broad between the ears. Viewed from the top, the skull is square. There is a deep median furrow that diminishes in depth from the stop to the occiput. Cheek muscles are prominent.

Muzzle: The muzzle is broad and thick with a very slight taper from the stop to the nose. The length of the muzzle is equal to 35 to 45 percent of the length of the head. Lips are moderately thick but not pendulous. The chin is well

The American Bulldog should have a complete set of large, evenly spaced, strong teeth. His large nose has wide nostrils; this dog's dark nose is a desirable color.

defined and must neither overlap the upper lip nor be covered by it.

Teeth: The American Bulldog has a complete set of large, evenly spaced white teeth. The preferred bite is undershot with the inside of the lower incisors extending in front of the upper incisors up to one-quarter inch. A scissors bite is acceptable. A level bite and extreme undershot bite are considered faults to the degree that the bite interferes with the dog's ability to work. Teeth are not visible when the mouth is closed. Worn teeth or broken teeth are acceptable. *Disqualification:* Overshot.

Nose: The nose is large with wide, open nostrils. The nose may be any color but darker pigment is preferred.

Eyes: Eyes are medium in size, round and set well apart. All colors are acceptable but brown is preferred. Haw is not visible. Dark eye rims are preferred. *Faults*: Very visible haws.

Ears: Ears may be cropped but natural ears are preferred. Natural ears are small to medium in size, high set, and may be drop, semi-prick or rose.

Drop ears: The ears are set high, level with the upper line of the skull, accentuating the skull's width. At the base, the ear is just slightly raised in front and then hangs along the cheek. The tip is slightly rounded. When pulled toward the eye, the ear should not extend past the outside corner of the eye.

Semi-prick ears: Same as drop ears except that only the tips of the ears drop forward.

Rose ears: Rose ears are small and set high on the skull. *Fault:* Hound ears.

NECK

The neck is where the American Bulldog exerts power to bring down livestock. The neck must be long enough to exert leverage, but short enough to exert power. The neck is muscular and, at its widest point, is nearly as broad as the head, with a slight arch at the crest, and tapering slightly from shoulders to the head. A slight dewlap is acceptable. *Faults:* Neck too short and thick; thin or weak neck.

The neck must be long enough to exert leverage, but short enough to exert power.

Forequarters

The shoulders are strong and well muscled. The shoulder blade is well laid back and forms, with the upper arm, an apparent 90-degree angle. The tips of the shoulder blades are set about 2 to 3 finger-widths apart.

The shoulders should be strong and well muscled, with legs parallel and strong.

The forelegs are heavily boned and very muscular. The elbows are set on a plane parallel to the body, neither close to the body nor turned out. Viewed from the front, the forelegs are perpendicular to the ground or may, especially in a dog with a very broad chest, incline slightly inward. The pasterns are short, powerful and slightly sloping when viewed in profile. Viewed from the front, the pasterns are straight.

The chest is deep and moderately wide with ample room for heart and lungs, and visible musculature.

Body

The chest is deep and moderately wide with ample room for heart and lungs. The ribs are well sprung from the spine and then flatten to form a deep body extending at least to the elbows, or lower in adult dogs. The topline inclines very slightly downward from well-developed withers to a broad muscular back. The loin is short, broad and slightly arched, blending into a moderately sloping croup. The flank is moderately tucked up and firm. *Serious faults:* Swayback; sloping topline.

Hindquarters

The hindquarters are well muscled and broad. The width and angulation of the hindquarters is in balance with the width and angulation of the forequarters. The thighs are well developed with thick, easily discerned muscles. The lower thighs are muscular and short. Viewed from the side, the rear pasterns are well let down and perpendicular to the ground. Viewed from the rear, the rear pasterns are straight and parallel to one another. *Faults:* Cowhocks; open hocks. *Serious faults:* Narrow or weak hindquarters.

Feet

The feet are round, medium in size, well arched and tight. *Fault:* Splayed feet. The seriousness of this fault is based on the amount of splay in the feet.

Tail

The American Bulldog may have a natural or a docked tail, but the natural tail is preferred. The natural tail is very thick at the base, and tapers to a point. The tail is set low. A "pump handle" tail is preferred but any tail carriage from upright, when the dog is excited, to relaxed between the hocks is acceptable. *Serious fault:* Tail curled over the back; corkscrew tail; upright tail when the dog is relaxed.

Coat

The coat is short, close and stiff to the touch. *Disqualifications:* Long or wavy coat.

More important than the height and weight is the dog's overall appearance of strength, agility and balance.

Color

Any color, color pattern or combination of colors is acceptable, except for solid black, solid blue and tricolor (white with patches of black and tan). Some dark brindle coats may appear black unless examined in very bright light. A buckskin color pattern, where the base of the hair is fawn and the tips are black, may also appear solid black. A judge should not disqualify an American Bulldog for black color unless the dog has been examined in sunlight or other equally bright light. *Disqualifications*: Solid

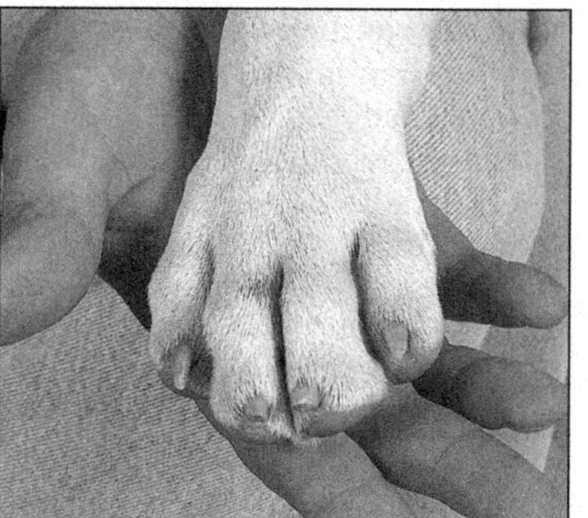

A well-developed foot of a young American Bulldog, rounded and tight.

The American Bulldog has quite a range in height and weight, depending upon gender and bloodline.

black with no white markings; tricolor (white with patches of black and tan).

Height and Weight

The American Bulldog must be sufficiently powerful and agile to chase, catch and bring down free-ranging livestock. Dogs capable of doing this come in a rather wide range of height and weight. Males are typically larger with heavier bone and more muscle than females. Both sexes, however, should have a well-balanced overall appearance.

Desirable height in a mature male ranges from 22 to 27 inches; in a mature female, from 20 to 25 inches. Desirable weight in a mature male ranges from 75 to 125 pounds; in a mature female, from 60 to 100 pounds.

In the UKC standard, any color, color pattern or combination of colors is acceptable except for solid black, solid blue and tricolor.

Gait

When trotting, the gait is effortless, smooth, powerful and well coordinated, showing good reach in front and drive behind. When moving, the backline remains level with only a slight flexing to indicate suppleness. Viewed from any position, legs turn neither in nor out, nor do feet cross or interfere with each other. As speed increases, feet tend to converge toward center line of balance.

Poor movement should be penalized to the degree to which it reduces the American Bulldog's ability to perform the tasks it was bred to do.

Disqualifications

Unilateral or bilateral cryptorchid. Viciousness or extreme shyness. Unilateral or bilateral deafness. Cowardice. Overshot. Long or wavy coat. Albinism. Solid black with no white markings. Tricolor (white with patches of black and tan).

EARS
Natural ears are preferred (left), though they may be cropped (right).

BITE
Acceptable bite is up to one-quarter inch undershot, shown here from front and side, or scissors.

FOREQUARTERS
Strong shoulders, heavily boned forelegs and a powerful appearance. Elbows parallel to body (left), neither too close nor turned out (right).

HINDQUARTERS
Well muscled and broad (left). Rear legs set directly under dog, angulation in balance with front angulation. Incorrect cowhocks shown on right.

BACK
Topline inclines very slightly downward from well-developed withers to a broad, muscular back (left). Swayback (right) is undesirable.

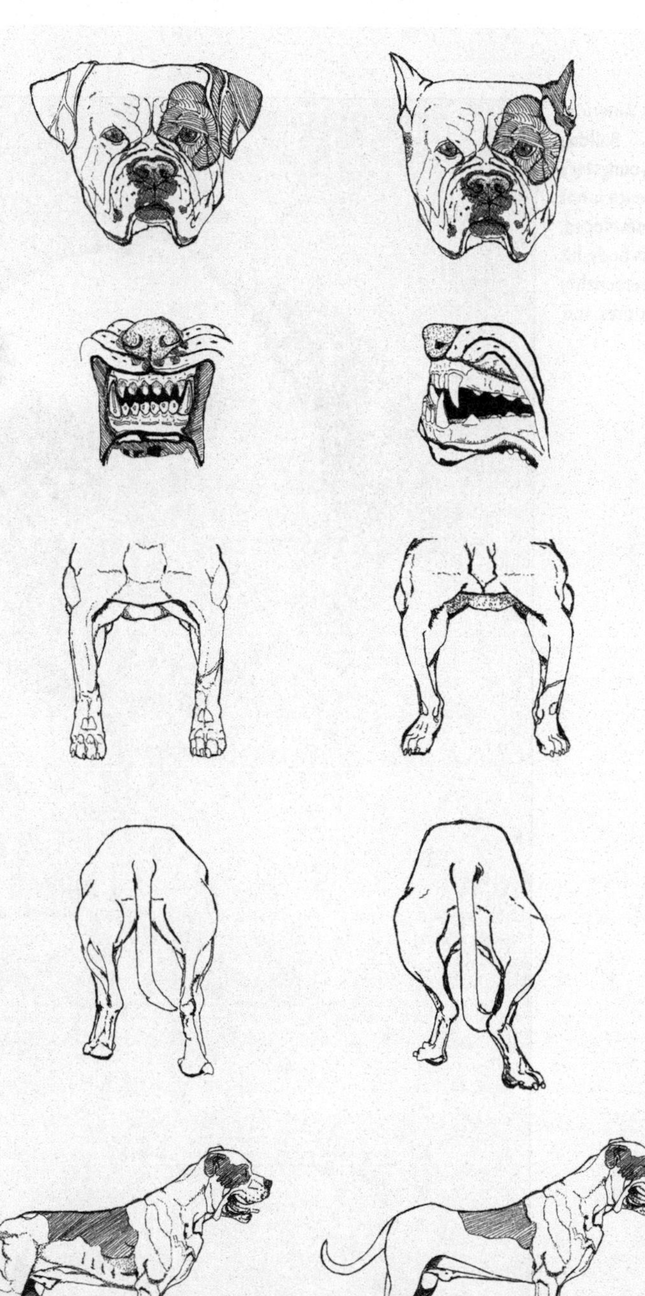

An American Bulldog youngster's confidence is not fully developed. Like his body, his personality matures, too.

Your Puppy

AMERICAN BULLDOG

ACQUIRING A PUPPY

Given the tremendous variation in lines of American Bulldogs, it's best for a potential owner to seek out a reputable breeder who is not selling huge dogs. The American Bulldog, at its ideal weight around 75 pounds, is a powerful, strong animal. Breeders who have created Bulldogs in excess of 100 pounds are not promoting true Bulldogs. Dogs of this size are not typical of the breed and may suffer from medical conditions not usually seen in the breed. The giant breeds (Mastiffs, Bullmastiffs, Neapolitan Mastiffs, etc.) can be prone to various bone cancers, hip dysplasia, etc., and have shorter life expectancies, and the same issues can occur in these atypical "oversized" American Bulldogs. In the case of the American Bulldog, size matters; smaller is indeed better. You are not purchasing a power tool, a utility vehicle or some other macho symbol where bigger is always better. There is nothing superior to an athletic, healthy, hardy 75-pound American Bulldog!

What could be cuter than an American Bulldog litter snuggled up for a snooze?

Color is a matter of personal choice, but whichever color you prefer, your puppy should have good pigment. Historically, the American Bulldog is a white dog or is predominantly white with patches of another color. The breeder should be able to predict the adult coloration, as the puppy color can change shade as he matures, though this is hardly something that gets too much attention in this breed. Dogs of other solid colors (such as fawn, brindle or black) may occur in lines of American Bulldogs. This is strictly a matter of preference, even though many fanciers do not

When selecting an American Bulldog puppy, you should opt for a sturdy well-built youngster that radiates good health and personality.

accept these as true American Bulldogs. In fact, the breed standards presented in this book do not accept black dogs.

Note the way your puppy prospect moves. The American Bulldog, even in puppyhood, should show deliberate movement with no tendency to stumble or drag the hind feet. This is not to say that a little puppy awkwardness isn't to be expected. Look at the mouth to make sure that the bite is fairly even, although maturity can often correct errors present in puppyhood. Undershot bites are very common in puppies and are to be avoided. If you have any doubts, ask to see the parents' mouths. As an adult, the bite should be only *slightly* undershot, if at all.

Inquire about inoculations and when the puppy was last dosed for worms. The breeder should be honest about the pup's health background, including hereditary health of the litter's parents and his line in general.

A COMMITTED NEW OWNER

By now you should understand what makes the American Bulldog a most unique and special dog, one that may fit nicely into your family and lifestyle. If you have researched breeders, you should be able to recognize a knowledgeable and responsible American Bulldog breeder who cares only about the integrity of the breed, the best interest of his pups and what kind of owner you will be.

A visit with the puppies and their breeder should be an education in itself. If your chosen breeder does not have pups available, you still should meet with him so the two of you can get to know each other. Breed research, breeder selection and puppy visitation are very important aspects of finding the puppy of your dreams. Beyond that, these

THE FAMILY TREE

Your puppy's pedigree is his family tree. Just as a child may resemble his parents and grandparents, so too will a puppy reflect the qualities, good and bad, of his ancestors, especially those in the first two generations. Therefore it's important to know as much as possible about a puppy's immediate relatives. Reputable and experienced breeders should be able to explain the pedigree and why they chose to breed from the particular dogs they used.

things also lay the foundation for a successful future with your pup. Puppy personalities within each litter vary, from the shy and easygoing puppy to the one who is dominant and assertive, with most pups falling somewhere in between. By spending time with the puppies, you will be able to recognize certain behaviors and what these behaviors indicate about each pup's temperament.

Which type of pup will complement your family dynamics is best determined by observing the puppies in action within their "pack." Your breeder's expertise and recommendations are also valuable. Although you may fall in love with a bold and brassy male, the breeder may suggest that another pup would be best for you. The breeder's experience in rearing American Bulldog pups and matching their temperaments with appropriate humans offers the best assurance that your pup will meet your needs and expectations. The type of puppy that you select is just as important as your decision that the American Bulldog is the breed for you.

The decision to live with a American Bulldog is a serious commitment and not one to be

HEALTH GUARANTEE

Your breeder may have offered a health guarantee. If not, do not feel awkward about asking for one as part of your sales agreement. An honest and reputable breeder will not be insulted. A health guarantee states that the breeder will take the pup back and give the buyer a refund if the vet discovers a problem. A health guarantee may also cover any hereditary diseases that show up before a certain age, in which case the breeder would provide a replacement. The exact terms will differ depending on what is discussed and should be put in writing between the breeder and the buyer; just make sure that you are in accord with the terms before you agree to purchase the pup and that you read all paperwork carefully.

White or almost completely white, with a sharply contrasting black nose, makes an attractive American Bulldog.

The new American Bulldog puppy requires housebreaking and training from his first day home to make him a well-behaved member of your family.

taken lightly. This puppy is a living sentient being that will be dependent on you for basic survival for his entire life. Beyond the basics of survival—food, water, shelter and protection—he needs much, much more. The new pup needs love, nurturing and a proper canine education to mold him into a responsible, well-behaved canine citizen. Your American Bulldog's health and good manners will need consistent monitoring and regular "tune-ups," so your job as a responsible dog owner will be ongoing throughout every stage of his life. If you are not prepared to accept these responsibilities and commit to them for the next decade, likely longer, then you are not prepared to own a dog of any breed.

Although the responsibilities of owning a dog may at times tax your patience, the joy of living with your American Bulldog far outweighs the workload, and a well-mannered adult dog is worth your time and effort. Before your very eyes, your new charge will grow up to be your most loyal friend, devoted to you unconditionally.

YOUR AMERICAN BULLDOG SHOPPING LIST

Just as expectant parents prepare a nursery for their baby, so should you ready your home for the arrival of your American Bulldog pup. If you have the necessary puppy supplies purchased and in place before he comes home, it will ease the puppy's transition from the warmth and familiarity of his mom and littermates to the brand-new environment of his

SIGNS OF A HEALTHY PUPPY

Healthy puppies are robust little fellows who are alert and active, sporting shiny coats and supple skin. They should not appear lethargic, bloated or pot-bellied, nor should they have flaky skin or runny or crusted eyes or noses. Their stools should be firm and well formed, with no evidence of blood or mucus.

new home and human family. You will be too busy to stock up and prepare your house after your pup comes home, that's for sure! Imagine how a pup must feel upon being transported to a strange new place. It's up to you to comfort him and to let your little pup know that he is going to be happy with you!

COST OF OWNERSHIP

The purchase price of your puppy is merely the first expense in the typical dog budget. Quality dog food, veterinary care (sickness and health maintenance), dog supplies and grooming costs will add up to big bucks every year. Can you adequately afford to support a canine addition to the family?

FOOD AND WATER BOWLS

Your puppy will need separate bowls for his food and water. Stainless steel bowls are generally preferred over plastic bowls since they sterilize better and pups are less inclined to chew on the metal. Heavy-duty ceramic bowls are popular, but consider how often you will have to pick up those heavy bowls! Buy adult-sized bowls, as your puppy will grow into them before you know it.

THE DOG CRATE

If you think that crates are tools of punishment and confinement

Though it may be hard to resist these adorable faces, you must make a carefully considered decision, making sure you get a sound, healthy pup whose personality is a good match with yours.

The pups will be fully weaned and started on a good-quality puppy-food diet before they leave for new homes.

for when a dog has misbehaved, think again. Most breeders and almost all trainers recommend a crate as the preferred house-training aid as well as for all-around puppy training and safety. Because dogs are natural den creatures that prefer cave-like environments, the benefits of crate use are many. The crate provides the puppy with his very own "safe house," a cozy place to sleep, take a break or seek comfort with a favorite toy; a travel aid to house your dog

when on the road, at motels or at the vet's office; a training aid to help teach your puppy proper toileting habits; a place of solitude when non-dog people happen to drop by and don't want a lively puppy—or even a well-behaved adult dog—saying hello or begging for attention.

Crates come in several types, although the wire crate and the fiberglass airline-type crate are the most popular. Both are safe and your puppy will adjust to either one, so the choice is up to you. The wire crates offer better visibility for the pup as well as better ventilation. Many of the wire crates easily fold down into suitcase-size carriers. The fiberglass crates, similar to those

FINDING A QUALIFIED BREEDER

Before you begin your puppy search, ask for references from your veterinarian, other breeders and perhaps other dog owners to refer you to someone they believe is reputable. Responsible breeders usually raise only one or two breeds of dog. Avoid any breeder who has several different breeds or has several litters at the same time. Dedicated breeders are usually involved with a breed or other dog club. Many participate in some sport or activity related to their breed. Just as you want to be assured of the breeder's qualifications, the breeder wants to be assured that you will make a worthy owner. Expect the breeder to interview you, asking questions about your goals for the pup, your experience with dogs and what kind of home you will provide.

used by the airlines for animal transport, are sturdier and more den-like. However, the fiberglass crates do not fold down and are less ventilated than the wire crates, which can be problematic in hot weather. Some of the newer crates are made of heavy plastic mesh; they are very lightweight and fold up into slim-line suitcases. However, a mesh crate might not be suitable for a pup with manic chewing habits.

Don't bother with a puppy-sized crate. Although your American Bulldog will be a small fellow when you bring him home, he will grow up in the blink of an eye and your puppy crate will be useless. Purchase a crate that will accommodate an adult American Bulldog. With such a range in sizes, it can be hard to predict your Bulldog's adult size, but if you've chosen your breeder well, you should have a good idea based on other dogs of his line. Regardless, any American Bulldog will require a large crate.

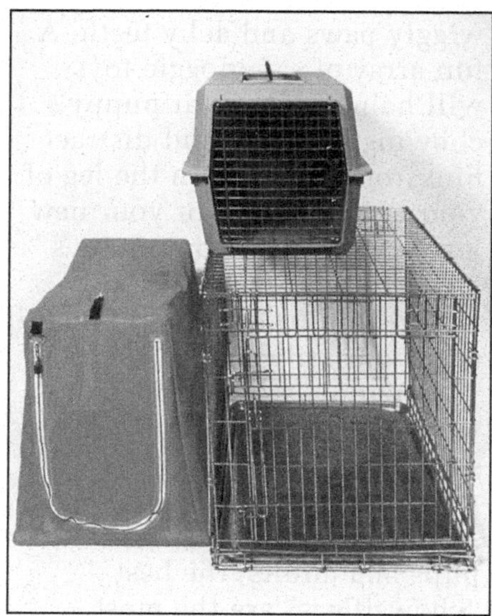

The three most common crate types: mesh on the left, wire on the right and fiberglass on top.

Bedding and Crate Pads

Your puppy will enjoy some type of soft bedding in his "room" (the crate), something he can snuggle into to feel cozy and secure. Old towels or blankets are good choices for a young pup, since he may (and probably will) have a toileting accident or two in the crate or decide to chew on the bedding material. Once he is fully trained and out of the early chewing stage, you can replace the puppy bedding with a permanent crate pad if you prefer. Crate pads and other dog beds run the gamut from inexpensive to high-end doggie-designer styles, but don't splurge on the good stuff until you are sure that your puppy is reliable and won't tear it up or make a mess on it.

Puppy Toys

Just as infants and older children require objects to stimulate their minds and bodies, puppies need toys to entertain their curious brains, wiggly paws and achy teeth. A fun array of safe doggie toys will help satisfy your puppy's chewing instincts and distract him from gnawing on the leg of your antique chair or your new leather sofa. Most puppy toys are cute and look as if they would be a lot of fun, but not all are necessarily safe or good for your puppy, so use caution when you go puppy-toy shopping.

American Bulldogs have strong powerful jaws. For older pups and adults, the best "chewcifiers" are the most durable nylon and rubber bones, designed specifically for hard-chewing breeds. Natural bones can splinter or develop dangerous sharp edges; pups and dogs can easily swallow or choke on those bone splinters. Veterinarians often tell of surgical nightmares involving bits of splintered bone, because in addition to the danger of choking, the sharp pieces can damage the intestinal tract.

Similarly, rawhide chews, while a favorite of most dogs and puppies, can be equally dangerous. Pieces of rawhide are easily swallowed after they get soft and gummy from chewing, and dogs have been known to choke on large pieces of ingested rawhide. Rawhide chews should be offered only when you can supervise and

TEETHING TIME

All puppies chew. It's normal canine behavior. Chewing just plain feels good to a puppy, especially during the three- to five-month teething period when the adult teeth are breaking through the gums. Rather than attempting to eliminate such a strong natural chewing instinct, you will be more successful if you redirect it and teach your puppy what he may or may not chew. Correct inappropriate chewing with a sharp "No!" and offer him a chew toy, praising him when he takes it. Don't become discouraged. Chewing usually decreases after the adult teeth have come in.

THE FAMILY FELINE

A resident cat has feline squatter's rights. The cat will treat the newcomer (your puppy) as she sees fit, regardless of what you do or say. So it's best to let the two of them work things out on their own terms. Cats have a height advantage and will generally leap to higher ground to avoid direct contact with a rambunctious pup. Some will hiss and boldly swat at a pup who passes by or tries to reach the cat. Keep the puppy under control in the presence of the cat, and they will eventually become accustomed to each other.

Here's a hint: move the cat's litter box where the puppy can't get into it! It's best to do so well before the pup comes home so the cat is used to the new location.

only for short time periods. Further, some dogs that show no other signs of aggression may find rawhide so irresistible that they become possessive over these chews.

Soft woolly toys are special puppy favorites during the teething period. They come in a wide variety of cute shapes and sizes; some look like little stuffed animals. Puppies love to shake them up and toss them about, or simply carry them around. Be careful of fuzzy toys that have button eyes or noses that your pup could chew off and swallow, and make sure that he does not disembowel a squeaky toy to remove the squeaker! Braided rope toys are similar in that they are fun to chew and toss around, but they shred easily and the strings are easy to swallow. The strings are not digestible and, if the puppy doesn't pass them in his stool, he could end up at the vet's office. As with rawhides, your Bulldog should be closely monitored with rope toys.

If you believe that your American Bulldog has ingested a piece of one of his toys, check his stools for the next couple of days to see if he passes the item when he defecates. At the same time, also watch for signs of intestinal distress. A call to your veterinarian might be in order to get his advice and be

Collaring Our Canines

The standard flat collar with a buckle or a snap, in leather, nylon or cotton, is widely regarded as the everyday all-purpose collar. If the collar fits correctly, you should be able to fit two fingers between the collar and the dog's neck.

Leather Buckle Collars

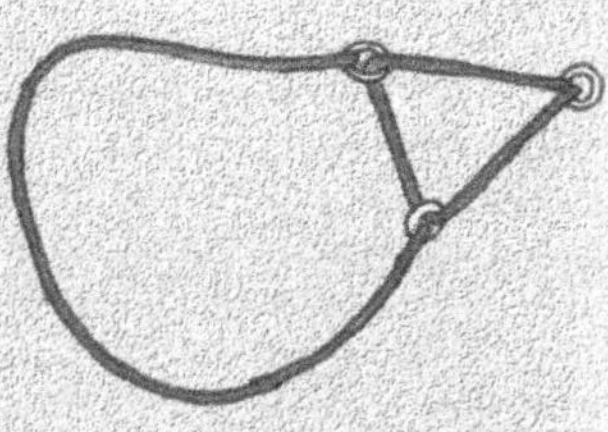

Limited-Slip Collar

The martingale, Greyhound or limited-slip collar is preferred by many dog owners and trainers. It is fixed with an extra loop that tightens when pressure is applied to the leash. The martingale collar gets tighter but does not "choke" the dog. The limited-slip collar should only be used for walking and training, not for free play or interaction with another dog. These types of collar should never be left on the dog, as the extra loop can lead to accidents.

Choke collars, usually made of stainless steel, are made for training purposes but are not recommended for small dogs or heavily coated breeds. The chains can injure small dogs or damage long/abundant coats. Thin nylon choke leads are commonly used on show dogs while in the ring, though they are not practical for everyday use.

Snap-Bolt Choke Collar

The harness, with two or three straps that attach over the dog's shoulders and around his torso, is a humane and safe alternative to the conventional collar. By and large, a well-made harness is virtually escape-proof. Harnesses are available in nylon and mesh and can be outfitted on most dogs, with chest girths ranging from 10 to 30 inches.

Harness

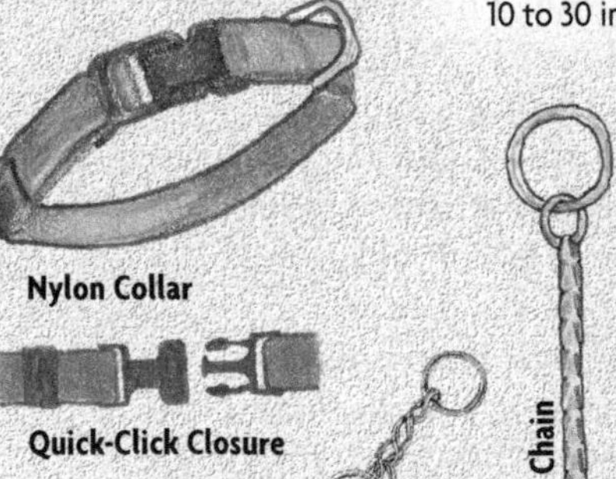

Nylon Collar

Quick-Click Closure

Snake Chain

Chrome Steel

Fur-Saver

Choke Chain Collars

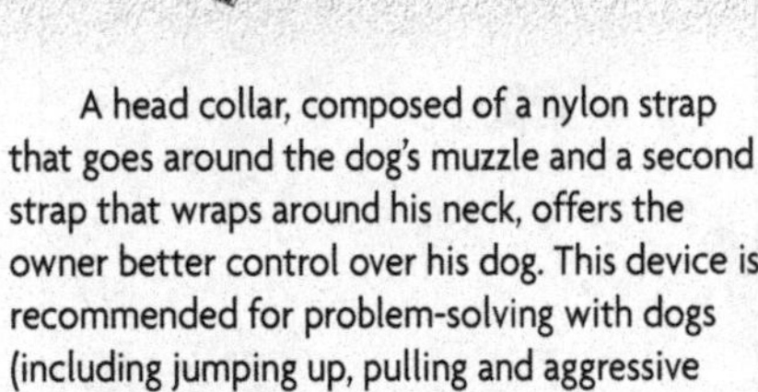

A head collar, composed of a nylon strap that goes around the dog's muzzle and a second strap that wraps around his neck, offers the owner better control over his dog. This device is recommended for problem-solving with dogs (including jumping up, pulling and aggressive behaviors), but must be used with care.

A training halter, including a flat collar and two straps, made of nylon and webbing, is designed for walking. There are several on the market; some are more difficult to put on the dog than others. The halter harness, with two small slip rings at each end, is recommended for ease of use.

on the safe side.

An all-time favorite toy for puppies (young and old!) is the empty gallon milk jug. Hard plastic juice containers—46 ounces or more—are also excellent. Such containers make lots of noise when they are batted about, and puppies go crazy with delight as they play with them. However, they don't often last more than a few minutes, so be sure to remove them when they get chewed up.

A word of caution about homemade toys: be careful with your choices of non-traditional play objects. Never use old shoes or socks, since a puppy cannot distinguish between the old ones on which he's allowed to chew and the new ones in your closet that are strictly off-limits. That principle applies to anything that resembles something that you don't want your puppy to chew.

Collars

A lightweight nylon collar is the best choice for a very young pup. Quick-clip collars are easy to put on and remove, and they can be adjusted as the puppy grows. Introduce him to his collar as soon as he comes home to get him accustomed to wearing it. He'll get used to it quickly and won't mind a bit. Make sure that it is snug enough that it won't slip off, yet loose

Start out with a sturdy collar for your Bulldog and adjust the size as necessary as the dog gets older, larger and stronger.

enough to be comfortable for the pup. You should be able to slip two fingers between the collar and his neck. Check the collar often, as puppies grow in spurts, and his collar can become too tight almost overnight. As the pup grows larger and stronger, he will need an accordingly thicker collar of nylon or perhaps leather. Training collars should never be used on a young puppy. Consult with a trainer before choosing a training collar for your American Bulldog.

Leashes

A 6-foot nylon lead is an excellent choice for a young puppy. It is lightweight and not as tempting to chew as a leather lead. You can switch to a 6-foot

Your local pet shop will have various sizes and strengths of collars and leads. An adult's requirements will differ from a pup's, just as show leads and collars differ from those for everyday use.

leather lead after your pup has grown and is used to walking politely on a lead. For initial puppy walks and house-training purposes, you should invest in a shorter lead so that you have more control over the puppy. At first, you don't want him wandering too far away from you and, when taking him out for toileting, you will want to keep him in the specific area chosen for his potty spot.

Once the puppy is heel-trained with a traditional leash, you can consider purchasing a retractable lead. A retractable lead is excellent for walking adult dogs that are already leash-wise. This type of lead allows the dog to roam farther away from you and explore a wider area when out walking, and also retracts when you need to keep him close to you. However, these leashes are made for specific weight ranges, so be sure to get one that can withstand your American Bulldogs's size. A too-light leash will break and be unsafe.

HOME SAFETY FOR YOUR PUPPY

The importance of puppy-proofing cannot be overstated. In addition to making your house comfortable for your American Bulldog's arrival, you also must make sure that your house is safe for your puppy before you bring him home. There are countless hazards in the owner's personal living environment that a pup can sniff, chew, swallow or destroy. Many are obvious; others are not. Do a thorough advance house check to remove or rearrange those things that could hurt your puppy, keeping any potentially dangerous items out of areas to which he will have access.

Electrical cords are especially dangerous, since puppies view them as irresistible chew toys. Unplug and remove all exposed cords or fasten them beneath a baseboard where the puppy cannot reach them. Veterinarians and

firefighters can tell you horror stories about electrical burns and house fires that resulted from puppy-chewed electrical cords. Consider this a most serious precaution for your puppy and the rest of your family.

Some dogs are more resistant to crate confinement, but any dog can be crate-trained with time and patience.

Scout your home for tiny objects that might be seen at a pup's eye level. Keep medication bottles and cleaning supplies well out of reach, and do the same with waste baskets and other trash containers. It goes without saying that you should not use rodent poison or other toxic chemicals in any puppy area and that you must

DON'T EAT THE DAISIES!

Many plants and flowers are beautiful to look at but can be highly toxic if ingested by your dog. Reactions range from abdominal pain and vomiting to convulsions and death. If the following plants are in your home, remove them. If they are outside your house or in your garden, avoid accidents by removing them or making sure your dog is never left unsupervised in those locations.

Azalea
Belladonna
Bird of paradise
Bulbs
Calla lily
Cardinal flower
Castor bean
Chinaberry tree
Daphne
Dumb cane
Dutchman's breeches
Elephant's ear
Hydrangea
Jack-in-the-pulpit
Jasmine
Jimsonweed
Larkspur
Laurel
Lily of the valley
Mescal bean
Mushrooms
Nightshade
Philodendron
Poinsettia
Prunus species
Tobacco
Yellow jasmine
Yews, *Taxus* species

A Dog-Safe Home

The dog-safety police are taking you on a house tour. Let's go room by room and see how safe your home is for your new pup. The following items are doggie dangers, so either they must be removed or the dog should be monitored or not allowed access to these areas.

Outdoors

- swimming pool
- pesticides
- toxic plants
- lawn fertilizers

Living Room

- house plants (some varieties are poisonous)
- fireplace or wood-burning stove
- paint on the walls (lead-based paint is toxic)
- lead drapery weights (toxic lead)
- lamps and electrical cords
- carpet cleaners or deodorizers

Bathroom

- blue water in the toilet bowl
- medicine cabinet (filled with potentially deadly bottles)
- soap bars, bleach, drain cleaners, etc.
- tampons

Kitchen

- household cleaners in the kitchen cabinets
- glass jars and canisters
- sharp objects (like kitchen knives, scissors and forks)
- garbage can (with remnants of good-smelling things like onions, potato skins, apple or pear cores, peach pits, coffee beans and other harmful tidbits)
- food left out on counters (some foods are toxic to dogs)

Garage

- antifreeze
- fertilizers (including rose foods)
- pesticides and rodenticides
- pool supplies (chlorine and other chemicals)
- oil and gasoline in containers
- sharp objects, electrical cords and power tools

PUPPY PARASITES

Parasites are nasty little critters that live in or on your dog or puppy. Most puppies are born with ascarid roundworms, which are acquired from dormant ascarids residing in the dam. Other parasites can be acquired through contact with infected fecal matter. Take a stool sample to your vet for testing. He will prescribe a safe wormer to treat any parasites found in your puppy's stool. Always have a fecal test performed at your dog's annual veterinary exam.

keep such containers safely locked up. You will be amazed at how many places a curious puppy can discover!

Once your house has cleared inspection, check your yard. A sturdy fence, well embedded into the ground, will give your dog a safe place to play and potty. Although American Bulldogs are not known to be escape artists, they are very athletic dogs, so at least a 6-foot-high fence will be required to contain an agile youngster or adult. Check the fence periodically for necessary repairs. If there is a weak link or space to squeeze through, a determined American Bulldog may become quite curious about getting through to the other side.

The garage and shed can be hazardous places for a pup, as things like fertilizers, chemicals and tools are usually kept there. It's best to keep these areas off-limits to the pup. Antifreeze is especially dangerous to dogs, as they find the taste appealing and it takes only a few licks from the driveway to kill a dog, puppy or adult, small breed or large.

VISITING THE VETERINARIAN

A good veterinarian is your American Bulldog puppy's best health-insurance policy. If you do not already have a vet, ask your breeder, friends and experienced dog people in your area for recommendations so that you can select a vet before you bring your American Bulldog puppy home. Also arrange for your puppy's first veterinary examination beforehand, since many vets do not have appointments available immediately and your puppy should visit the vet within a day or so of coming home.

Never permit your puppy to choose his own "toys." A common item like a sponge used for cleaning might contain chemicals that could be very dangerous to the puppy.

It's important to make sure that your puppy's first visit to the vet is a pleasant and positive one. The vet should take great care to befriend the pup and handle him gently to make their first meeting a positive experience. The vet will give the pup a thorough physical examination and set up a schedule for vaccinations and other necessary wellness visits. Be sure to show your vet any health and inoculation records, which you should have received from your breeder. Your vet is a great source of canine health information, so be sure to ask questions and take notes. Creating a health journal for your puppy will make a handy reference for his wellness and any future health problems that may arise.

Cuddling with and handling your new pup will help the two of you form a bond when he first comes home.

MEETING THE FAMILY

Your American Bulldog's homecoming is an exciting time for all members of the family, and it's only natural that everyone will be eager to meet him, pet him and play with him. However, for the puppy's sake, it's best to make these initial family meetings as uneventful as possible so that the pup is not overwhelmed with too much too soon. Remember, he has just left his dam and his littermates and is away from the breeder's home for the first time. He is apprehensive and wondering where he is and who all these strange humans are. It's best to let him explore on his own and meet the family members as he feels comfortable. Let him investigate all the new smells, sights and sounds at his own pace. Children should be especially careful to not get overly excited, use loud voices or hug the pup too tightly. Be calm, gentle and affectionate, and be ready to comfort him if he appears frightened or uneasy.

Be sure to show your puppy his new crate during this first

day home. Toss a treat or two inside the crate; if he associates the crate with food, he will associate the crate with good things. If he is comfortable with the crate, you can offer him his first meal inside it. Leave the door ajar so he can wander in and out as he chooses.

FIRST NIGHT IN HIS NEW HOME

So much has happened in your American Bulldog puppy's first day away from the breeder. He's had his first car ride to his new home. He's met his new human family and perhaps the other family pets. He has explored his new house and yard, at least those places where he is to be allowed during his first weeks at home. He may have visited his new veterinarian. He has eaten his first meal or two away from his dam and littermates. Surely that's enough to tire out an eight-week-old American Bulldog pup...or so you hope!

> **CONFINEMENT**
>
> It is wise to keep your puppy confined to a small "puppy-proofed" area of the house for his first few weeks at home. Gate or block off a space near the door he will use for outdoor potty trips. Expandable baby gates are useful to create puppy's designated area. If he is allowed to roam through the entire house or even only several rooms, it will be more difficult to house-train him.

Sturdy rope toys are usually favorites of dogs of all ages.

It's bedtime. During the day, the pup investigated his crate, which is his new den and sleeping space, so it is not entirely strange to him. Line the crate with a soft towel or blanket that he can snuggle into and gently place him into the crate for the night. Some breeders send home a piece of bedding from where the pup slept with his littermates, and those familiar scents are a great comfort for the puppy on his first night without his siblings.

He will probably whine or cry. The puppy is objecting to the confinement and the fact that he is alone for the first time. This can be a stressful time for you as well as for the pup. It's important that you remain strong and don't let the puppy out of his crate to

A good breeder puts time into the pups' early socialization, making it easier for them to leave the puppy pack and become part of a human family.

comfort him. He will fall asleep eventually. If you release him, the puppy will learn that crying means "out" and will continue that habit. You are laying the groundwork for future habits. Some breeders find that soft music can soothe a crying pup and help him get to sleep.

The new Bulldog puppy requires gentle petting and verbal assurance. This is "getting to know you" time!

SOCIALIZING YOUR PUPPY

The first 20 weeks of your American Bulldog puppy's life are the most important of his entire lifetime. A properly socialized puppy will grow up to be a confident and stable adult who will be a pleasure to live with and a welcome addition to the neighborhood.

The importance of socialization cannot be overemphasized. Research on canine behavior has proven that puppies who are not exposed to new sights, sounds, people and animals during their first 20 weeks of life will grow up to be timid and fearful, even aggressive, and unable to flourish outside of their home environment.

Socializing your puppy is not difficult and, in fact, will be a fun time for you both. Lead training goes hand in hand with socialization, so your puppy will be learning how to walk on a lead at the same time that he's meeting the neighborhood. Because the American Bulldog is such a terrific breed, everyone

will enjoy meeting "the new kid on the block." Take him for short walks, to the park and to other dog-friendly places where he will encounter new people, especially children. Puppies automatically recognize children as "little people" and are drawn to play with them. Just make sure that you supervise these meetings and that the children do not get too rough or encourage him to play too hard. An overzealous pup can often nip too hard, frightening the child and in turn making the puppy overly excited. A bad experience in puppyhood can impact a dog for life, so a pup that has a negative experience with a child may grow up to be shy or even aggressive around children.

Take your puppy along on your daily errands. Puppies are natural "people magnets," and most people who see your pup will want to pet him. All of these encounters will help to mold him into a confident adult dog. Likewise, you will soon feel like a confident, responsible dog owner, rightly proud of your well-mannered American Bulldog.

Be especially careful of your puppy's encounters and experiences during the eight-to-ten-week-old period, which is also called the "fear period." This is a serious imprinting period, and all contact during this time should be gentle and positive. A frightening or negative event could leave a permanent impression that could affect his future behavior if a similar situation arises.

Also make sure that your puppy has received his first and second rounds of vaccinations before you expose him to other

GETTING ACQUAINTED

When visiting a litter, ask the breeder for suggestions on how best to interact with the puppies. If possible, get right into the middle of the pack and sit down with them. Observe which pups climb into your lap and which ones shy away. Toss a toy for them to chase and bring back to you. It's easy to fall in love with the puppy who picks you, but keep your future objectives in mind before you make your final decision.

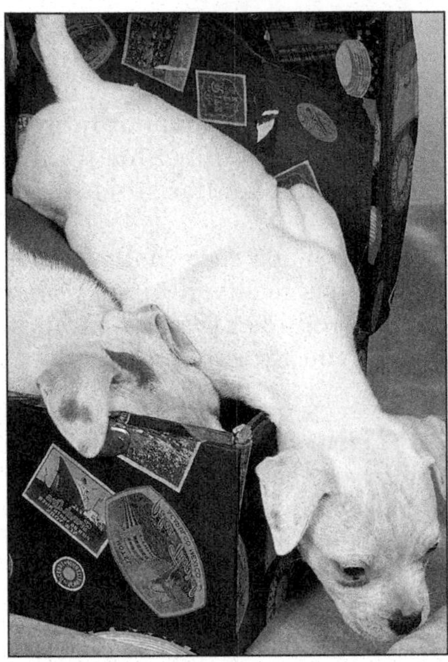

Do not leave handbags, luggage, etc., accessible to Bulldog puppies. They are very inquisitive, to say nothing of the unintentional damage their teeth can do.

dogs or bring him to places that other dogs may frequent. Avoid dog parks and other strange-dog areas until your vet assures you that your puppy is fully immunized and resistant to the diseases that can be passed

A puppy can use those pleading eyes to try to get his way!

between canines. Discuss socialization with your breeder, as some breeders recommend socializing the puppy even before he has received all of his inoculations, depending on how outgoing the breed or puppy may be. Early socialization with other dogs is very important with the American Bulldog to prevent dog aggression.

LEADER OF THE PUPPY'S PACK

Like other canines, your puppy needs an authority figure, someone he can look up to and regard as the leader of his "pack." His first pack leader was his dam, who taught him to be polite and not chew too hard on her ears or nip at her muzzle. He learned those same lessons from his littermates. If he played too rough, they cried in pain and stopped the game, which sent an important message to the rowdy puppy.

As puppies play together, they are also struggling to determine who will be the boss. Being pack animals, dogs need someone to be in charge. If a litter of puppies remained together beyond puppyhood, one of the pups would emerge as the strongest one, the one who calls the shots.

Once your puppy leaves the pack, he will look intuitively for a new leader. If he does not recognize you as that leader, he will try to assume that position for himself. Of course, it is hard to imagine your adorable American Bulldog puppy trying to be in charge when he is so small and seemingly helpless. You must remember that these are natural canine instincts. Do not cave in and allow your pup to get the upper "paw"!

Just as socialization is so important during these first 20 weeks, so too is your puppy's early education. He was born without any bad habits. He does not know what is good or bad behavior. If he does things like nipping and digging, it's because he is having fun and doesn't know that humans consider these things as "bad." It's your job to teach him proper puppy manners, and this is the best time to accomplish that...before he has developed bad habits, since it is much more difficult to "unlearn" or correct unacceptable learned behavior than to teach good behavior from the start.

Make sure that all members of the family understand the importance of being consistent when training their new puppy. If you tell the puppy to stay off the sofa and your daughter allows him to cuddle on the couch to watch her favorite television show, your pup will be confused about what he is

CREATE A SCHEDULE

Puppies thrive on sameness and routine. Offer meals at the same time each day, take him out at regular times for potty trips and do the same for play periods and outdoor activity. Make note of when your puppy naps and when he is most lively and energetic, and try to plan his day around those times. Once he is house-trained and more predictable in his habits, he will be better able to tolerate changes in his schedule.

KEEP OUT OF REACH

Most dogs don't browse around your medicine cabinet, but accidents do happen! The drug acetaminophen, the active ingredient in certain popular pain-relievers, can be deadly to dogs and cats if ingested in large quantities. Acetaminophen toxicity, caused by the dog's swallowing 15 to 20 tablets, can be manifested in abdominal pains within a day or two of ingestion, as well as liver damage. If you suspect your dog has swiped a bottle of pills, get the dog to the vet immediately so that the vet can induce vomiting and cleanse the dog's stomach.

and is not allowed to do. Have a family conference before your pup comes home so that everyone understands the basic principles of puppy training and the rules you have set forth for the pup, and agrees to follow them.

A curious puppy should be allowed to explore his new surroundings, under your watchful eye, of course.

The old saying that "an ounce of prevention is worth a pound of cure" is especially true when it comes to puppies. It is much easier to prevent inappropriate behavior than it is to change it. It's also easier and less stressful for the pup, since it will keep discipline to a minimum and create a more positive learning environment for him. That, in turn, will also be easier on you!

Here are a few commonsense tips to keep your belongings safe and your puppy out of trouble:

- Keep your closet doors closed and your shoes, socks and other apparel off the floor so your puppy can't get at them.
- Keep a secure lid on the trash container or put the trash where your puppy can't dig into it. He can't damage what he can't reach!
- Supervise your puppy at all times to make sure he is not getting into mischief. If he starts to chew the corner of the rug, you can distract him instantly by tossing a toy for him to fetch. You also will be able to whisk him outside when you notice that he is about to piddle on the carpet. If you can't see your puppy, you can't teach him or correct his behavior.

SOLVING PUPPY PROBLEMS

Chewing and Nipping

Nipping at fingers and toes is normal puppy behavior. Chewing is also the way that puppies investigate their surroundings. However, you will have to teach your puppy that chewing anything other than his toys is not acceptable. That won't happen overnight and at times puppy teeth will test your patience. However, if you allow nipping and chewing to continue, just think about the damage that a mature American Bulldog can do with a full set of adult teeth. You do not want to take a chance with an American Bulldog, as this is a dog whose jaws become naturally very strong.

Whenever your puppy nips your hand or fingers, cry out "Ouch!" in a loud voice, which should startle your puppy and stop him from nipping, even if only for a moment. Immediately distract him by offering a small treat or an appropriate toy for him to chew instead (which means having chew toys and puppy treats handy or in your pockets at all times). Praise him when he takes the toy and tell him what a good fellow he is. Praise is just as or even more important in puppy training as discipline and correction.

Pet shops have many toys from which you can select. You will need plenty of safe toys to properly direct a teething pup's chewing energy.

Puppies also tend to nip at children more often than adults, since they perceive little ones to be more vulnerable and more similar to their littermates. Teach your children appropriate responses to nipping behavior. If they are unable to handle it themselves, you may have to intervene. Puppy nips can be quite painful and a child's frightened reaction will only encourage a puppy to nip harder, which is a natural

Puppies love to chew on footwear, and it doesn't matter if someone's foot is inside it! Nipping at shoes and shoelaces should always be discouraged.

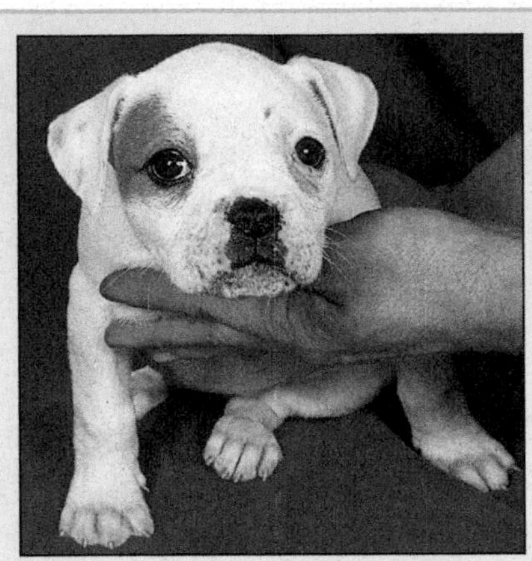

NEW RELEASES
Most breeders release their puppies between eight and ten weeks of age. A breeder who allows puppies to leave the litter at five or six weeks of age may be more concerned with profit than with the puppies' welfare. However, some breeders of show or working breeds may hold one or more top-quality puppies longer, occasionally until three or four months of age, in order to evaluate the puppies' career or show potential and decide which one(s) they will keep for themselves.

canine response. As with all other puppy situations, interaction between your American Bulldog puppy and children should be supervised.

Chewing on objects, not just family members' fingers and ankles, is also normal canine behavior that can be especially tedious (for the owner, not the pup) during the teething period when the puppy's adult teeth are coming in. At this stage, chewing just plain feels good. Furniture legs and cabinet corners are common puppy favorites. Shoes and other personal items also taste pretty good to a pup.

The best solution is, once again, prevention. If you value something, keep it tucked away and out of reach. You can't hide your dining-room table in a closet, but you can try to deflect the chewing by applying a bitter product made just to deter dogs from chewing. Available in a spray or cream, this substance is vile-tasting, although safe for dogs, and most puppies will avoid the forbidden object after one tiny taste. You also can apply the product to your leather leash if the puppy tries to chew on his lead during leash-training sessions.

Keep a ready supply of safe chews handy to offer your American Bulldog as a distraction when he starts to chew on something that's a "no-no." Remember, at this tender age he does not yet know what is permitted or forbidden, so you have to be "on call" every minute he's awake and on the prowl.

You may lose a treasure or two during puppy's growing-up period, and the furniture could sustain a nasty nick or two. These can be trying times, so be prepared for those inevitable accidents and comfort yourself in knowing that this too shall pass.

"Counter Surfing"

What we like to call "counter surfing" usually starts to happen as soon as a puppy realizes that he is big enough to stand on his hind legs and investigate the good stuff on the kitchen counter or the coffee table. Once again, you have to be there to prevent it! As soon as you see your American Bulldog even start to raise himself up, startle him with a sharp "No!" or "Aaahh, aaahh!" If he succeeds and manages to get one or both paws on the forbidden surface, remove his paws from the surface as you tell him "Off" and place his feet back on the ground. As soon as he's back on all four paws, command him to sit and praise at once.

For surf prevention, make sure to keep any tempting treats or edibles out of reach, where your American Bulldog can't see or smell them. It's the old rule of prevention yet again.

Food Guarding

Some dogs are picky eaters; others seem to inhale their food without chewing it. Occasionally, the true "chow hound" will become protective of his food, which is one dangerous step toward other aggressive behavior. Food guarding is obvious: your puppy will growl, snarl or even attempt to bite you if you approach his food bowl or put your hand into his pan while he's eating.

This behavior is not acceptable, and very preventable! If your puppy is an especially voracious eater, sit next to him occasionally while he eats and dangle your fingers in his food bowl. Don't feed him in a corner, where he could feel possessive of his eating space. Rather, place his food bowl in an open area of your kitchen where you are in close proximity. Occasionally remove his food in mid-meal, tell him he's a good boy and return his bowl.

If your pup becomes possessive of his food, look for other signs of future aggression, like guarding his favorite toys or refusing to obey obedience commands that he knows. Consult an obedience trainer for help in reinforcing obedience so that your American Bulldog will fully understand that *you* are the boss.

Puppyhood is the time to expose your American Bulldog to other dogs—other dog-friendly dogs, that is.

Proper Care of Your

AMERICAN BULLDOG

Adding an American Bulldog to your household means adding a new family member who will need your care each and every day. When your American Bulldog pup first comes home, you will start a routine with him so that, as he grows up, your dog will have a daily schedule just as you do. The aspects of your dog's daily care will likewise become regular parts of your day, so you'll both have a new schedule. Dogs learn by consistency and thrive on routine: regular times for meals, exercise, grooming and potty trips are just as important for your dog as they are for you! Your dog's schedule will depend much on your family's daily routine, but remember that you now have a new member of the family who is part of your day every day!

The easiest way to feed a puppy is to start out with the same food that he was fed by the breeder.

FEEDING

Feeding your dog the best diet is based on various factors, including age, activity level, overall condition and size of breed. When you visit the breeder, he will share with you his advice about the proper diet for your dog based on his experience with the breed and the foods with which he has had success. Likewise, your vet will be a helpful source of advice throughout the dog's life and will aid you in planning a diet for optimal health.

FEEDING THE PUPPY

Of course, your pup's very first food will be his dam's milk. There may be special situations in which pups fail to nurse, necessitating that the breeder hand-feed them with a formula, but for the most part pups spend the first weeks of life nursing from their dam. The breeder weans the pups by gradually introducing solid foods and decreasing the milk meals. Pups may even start themselves off on the weaning process, albeit inadvertently, if they snatch bites from their mom's food bowl.

By the time the pups are ready for new homes, they are fully weaned and eating a good puppy food. As a new owner, you may be thinking, "Great! The breeder has taken care of the hard part." Not so fast.

A puppy's first year of life is the time when all or most of his growth and development takes place. This is a delicate time, and diet plays a huge role in proper skeletal and muscular formation. Improper diet and exercise habits

Hopefully this eager American Bulldog won't be disappointed when he finds out it's just a toy!

can lead to damaging problems that will compromise the dog's health and movement for his entire life. That being said, new owners should not worry needlessly. With the myriad types of food formulated specifically for growing pups of different-sized breeds, dog-food manufacturers have taken much of the guesswork out of feeding your puppy well. Since growth-food formulas are designed to provide the nutrition

SWITCHING FOODS

There are certain times in a dog's life when it becomes necessary to switch his food; for example, from puppy to adult food and then from adult to senior-dog food. Additionally, you may decide to feed your pup a different type of food from what he received from the breeder, and there may be "emergency" situations in which you can't find your dog's normal brand and have to offer something else temporarily. Anytime a change is made, for whatever reason, the switch must be done gradually. You don't want to upset the dog's stomach or end up with a picky eater who refuses to eat something new. A tried-and-true approach is, over the course of about a week, to mix a little of the new food in with the old, increasing the proportion of new to old as the days progress. At the end of the week, you'll be feeding his regular portions of the new food, and he will barely notice the change.

that a growing puppy needs, it is unnecessary and, in fact, can prove harmful to add supplements to the diet. Research has shown that too much of certain vitamin supplements and minerals predispose a dog to skeletal problems. It's by no means a case of "if a little is good, a lot is better." At every stage of your dog's life, too much or too little in the way of nutrients can be harmful, which is why a manufactured complete food is the easiest way to know that your dog is getting what he needs.

Because of a young pup's small body and accordingly small digestive system, his daily portion will be divided up into small meals throughout the day. This can mean starting off with three or more meals a day and decreasing the number of meals as the pup matures. For the adult, it is generally thought that dividing the day's food into two meals on a morning/evening schedule is healthier for the dog's digestion than one large daily portion. American Bulldogs can be kept on a puppy diet up to about 18 months of age, even up to two years of age, as this is a slow-maturing breed.

Regarding the feeding schedule, feeding the pup at the same times and in the same place each day is important for both housebreaking purposes and establishing the dog's everyday routine. As for the amount to feed, growing puppies generally need proportionately more food per body weight than their adult counterparts, but a pup should never be allowed to gain excess weight. Dogs of all ages should be kept in proper body condition, but extra weight can strain a pup's developing frame, causing skeletal problems.

DIET DON'TS

- Got milk? Don't give it to your dog! Dogs cannot tolerate large quantities of cow's milk, as they do not have the enzymes to digest lactose.
- You may have heard of dog owners who add raw eggs to their dogs' food for a shiny coat or to make the food more palatable, but consumption of raw eggs too often can cause a deficiency of the vitamin biotin.
- Avoid feeding table scraps, as they will upset the balance of the dog's complete food. Additionally, fatty or highly seasoned foods can cause upset canine stomachs.
- Do not offer raw meat to your dog. Raw meat can contain parasites; it also is high in fat.
- Vitamin A toxicity in dogs can be caused by too much raw liver, especially if the dog already gets enough vitamin A in his balanced diet, which should be the case.
- Bones like chicken, pork chop and other soft bones are not suitable, as they easily splinter.

Watch your pup's weight as he grows and, if the recommended amounts seem to be too much or too little for your pup, consult the vet about appropriate dietary changes. Keep in mind that treats, although small, can quickly add up throughout the day, contributing unnecessary calories. Treats are fine when used prudently; opt for dog treats specially formulated to be healthy or for nutritious snacks like small pieces of cheese or cooked chicken.

NOT HUNGRY?

No dog in his right mind would turn down his dinner, would he? If you notice that your dog has lost interest in his food, there could be any number of causes. Dental problems are a common cause of appetite loss, one that is often overlooked. If your dog has a toothache, a loose tooth or sore gums from infection, chances are it doesn't feel so good to chew. Think about when you've had a toothache! If your dog does not approach the food bowl with his usual enthusiasm, look inside his mouth for signs of a problem. Whatever the cause, you'll want to consult your vet so that your chow hound can get back to his happy, hungry self.

Feeding the Adult Dog

For the adult (meaning physically mature) dog, feeding properly is about maintenance, not growth. Again, correct weight is a concern. Your dog should appear fit and should have an evident "waist." His ribs should not be protruding (a sign of being underweight), but they should be covered by only a slight layer of fat. Under normal circumstances, an adult dog can be maintained fairly easily with a high-quality nutritionally complete adult-formula food.

Factor treats into your dog's overall daily caloric intake, and avoid offering table scraps. Some "people foods," including chocolate, onions, grapes, raisins and nuts, are actually toxic to dogs, while feeding from the table encourages begging and overeating. Overweight dogs are more prone to health problems. Research has even shown that obesity takes years off a dog's life. With that in mind, resist the urge to overfeed and over-treat. Don't make unnecessary additions to

You will get to know the daily portions that maintain your adult American Bulldog in good condition.

your dog's diet, whether with tidbits or with extra vitamins and minerals.

The amount of food needed for proper maintenance will vary depending on the individual dog's activity level, but you will be able to tell whether the daily portions are keeping him in good shape. With the wide variety of good complete foods available, choosing what to feed is largely a matter of personal preference. Just as with the puppy, the adult dog should have consistency in his mealtimes and feeding place. This keeps the daily routine consistent and allows the owner to implement preventive measures against the deadly gastric torsion (bloat), explained in more detail in the health chapter. Regular mealtimes also allow the owner to see how much his dog is eating. If the dog seems never to be satisfied or, likewise, becomes uninterested in his food, the owner will know right away that something is wrong and can consult the vet.

Diets for the Aging Dog

A good rule of thumb is that once a dog has reached 75% of his expected lifespan, he has reached "senior citizen" or geriatric status. Your American Bulldog will be considered a senior at about 7 or 8 years of age; based on his size, he has an average lifespan of about 10–12 years, although the breed certainly can live longer. (The smallest breeds generally enjoy the longest lives and the largest breeds have shorter lifespans.)

What does aging have to do with your dog's diet? No, he won't get a discount at the local diner's early-bird special. Yes, he will require some dietary changes to accommodate the changes that come along with increased age. One change is that the older dog's dietary needs become more similar to that of a puppy. Specifically, dogs can metabolize more protein as youngsters and seniors than in the adult-maintenance stage. Discuss with your vet whether you need to switch to a higher-protein or senior-formulated food or whether your current adult-dog food contains sufficient nutrition for the senior.

Watching the dog's weight remains essential, even more so in the senior stage. Older dogs are already more vulnerable to illness, and obesity only contributes to their susceptibility to problems. As the older dog becomes less active and thus exercises less, his regular portions may cause him to gain weight. At this point, you may consider decreasing his daily food intake or switching to a reduced-calorie food. As with other changes, you should consult your vet for advice.

DON'T FORGET THE WATER!

Regardless of what type of food your dog eats, there's no doubt that he needs plenty of water. Water is essential for hydration and proper body function just as it is in humans. Fresh cold water, in a clean bowl, should be made available to your dog. There are special circumstances, such as during puppy housebreaking, when you will want to monitor your pup's water intake so that you will be able to predict when he will need to relieve himself, but water must be available to him nonetheless. Also, as some vets have recommended, do not leave water bowls down when feeding your American Bulldog. Limiting his water intake at mealtimes and never allowing him to gulp water at any time can help guard your dog against bloat.

You will get to know how much your dog typically drinks in a day. Of course, in the heat or if exercising vigorously, he will be more thirsty and will drink more. However, if he begins to drink noticeably more water for no apparent reason, this could signal any of various problems, and you are advised to consult your vet.

Water is the best drink for dogs. Some owners are tempted to give milk from time to time or to moisten dry food with milk, but dogs do not have the enzymes necessary to digest the lactose in milk, which is much different from the milk that nursing puppies receive. Therefore, stick with clean fresh water to quench your dog's thirst, and always have it readily available to him.

EXERCISE

Exercising an American Bulldog is not as daunting as it may seem. The American Bulldog is a working dog, not a field dog that has pent-up energy or a track dog that has long legs to stretch. Nonetheless, he needs exercise and will enjoy spending active time with you. Just as with anything else you do with your dog, you must set a routine for his

PUPPY STEPS

Puppies are brimming with activity and enthusiasm. It seems that they can play all day and night without tiring, but don't overdo your puppy's exercise regimen. Easy does it for at least the puppy's first nine months. Keep walks brief and don't let the puppy engage in stressful jumping games. The puppy frame is delicate, and too much exercise during those critical growing months can cause injury to his bone structure, ligaments and musculature. Save his first jog for his first birthday!

EXTRA SUMMER STRESS

Certain dogs encounter more difficulties in the heat and humidity than others; these include young puppies, senior dogs, obese dogs and dogs with short faces (such as your American Bulldog). Likewise, if your dog is in poor physical condition or suffering from illness, the heat will take more of a toll on him. Dogs that spend most of their time in the cool climate of air-conditioned homes will be less accustomed to heat and have more problems adjusting. Keep an eye on your American Bulldog in hot weather, and schedule his exercise times during the cooler morning and evening hours.

exercise. It's the same as your daily run before work or never missing the 7 p.m. aerobics class. If you plan it and get into the habit of actually doing it, it will become just another part of your day. Think of it as making daily exercise appointments with your dog, and stick to your schedule.

As a rule, dogs in normal health should have at least a half-hour of activity each day. Dogs with health or orthopedic problems may have specific limitations, so their exercise plans are best devised with the help of a vet. For healthy dogs, there are many ways to fit 30 minutes of activity into your day. Depending on your schedule, you may plan a 15-minute walk or activity session in the morning and again in the evening, or do it all at once in a half-hour session each day. No matter your schedule, plan for ample time for your dog to rest before and after exercise and mealtimes. Walking is the most popular way to exercise a dog (it's good for you, too!); other suggestions include retrieving games, jogging and disc-catching or other active games with his toys. If you have a safe body of water nearby and a dog that likes to swim, swimming is an excellent form of exercise for dogs, putting no stress on their frames.

For overweight dogs, dietary changes and activity will help the goal of weight loss. (Sound familiar?) While they should of course be encouraged to be active, remember not to overdo it, as the excess weight is already putting strain on his vital organs and bones. As for highly active dogs, some of them never seem to tire! They will enjoy time spent with their owners doing things together.

Regardless of your dog's condition and activity level, exercise offers benefits to all dogs and owners. Consider the fact that dogs who are kept active are more stimulated both physically and mentally, meaning that they are less likely to become bored and lapse into destructive behavior. Also consider the benefits of one-on-one time with your dog every day, continually strengthening the bond between the two of you. Furthermore, exercising together will improve health and longevity for both of you. You both need exercise, and now you and your dog have a workout partner and motivator!

GROOMING

BRUSHING

A natural bristle brush, a slicker brush or even a hound glove can be used for regular routine brushing. Grooming is effective for removing dead hair and stimulating the dog's natural oils to add shine and a healthy look to the coat. Your American Bulldog is not a breed that needs excessive grooming, but his coat needs to be brushed every few days as part of routine maintenance. Regular brushing will get rid of dust and dandruff and remove any dead hair. Regular grooming sessions are also a good way to spend time with your dog. Many dogs grow to like the feel of being brushed and will enjoy the routine.

BATHING

In general, dogs need to be bathed only a few times a year, possibly more often if your dog gets into something messy or if he starts to smell like a dog. Show dogs are usually bathed before every show, which could be as frequently as weekly, although this depends on the owner. Bathing too frequently can have negative effects on the skin and coat, removing natural oils and causing dryness.

If you give your dog his first bath when he is young, he will become accustomed to the process. Wrestling a dog into the tub or chasing a freshly shampooed dog who has escaped from the bath will be no fun! Most dogs don't naturally enjoy their baths, but you at least want yours to cooperate with you.

Before bathing the dog, have the items you'll need close at hand. First, decide where you will bathe the dog. You should have a tub or basin with a non-slip surface. In warm weather, some like to use a portable pool in the yard, although you'll want to make sure your dog doesn't head for the nearest dirt pile following his bath! You will also need a hose or shower spray to wet the coat thoroughly, a shampoo formulated for dogs and several absorbent towels. Human shampoos are too harsh for dogs' coats and will dry them out.

Before wetting the dog, give

Your American Bulldog's sleek coat doesn't need much grooming, but he may need a bath once in a while if his time outdoors leaves his coat less than white.

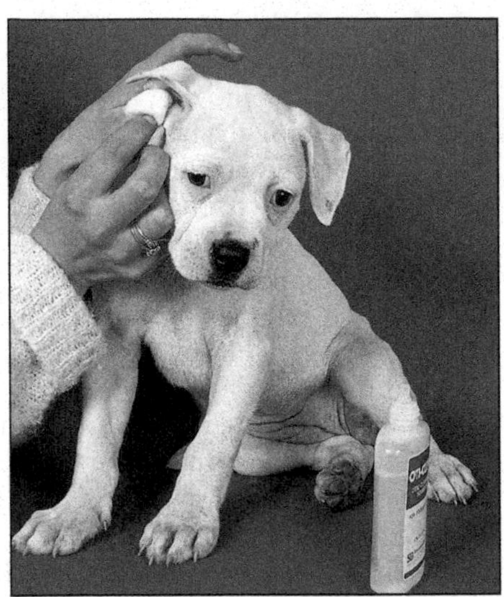

Ear cleaning is an important part of your grooming routine. Use soft cotton to clean gently, *never* probing into the ear canal.

him a brush-through to remove any dead hair and dirt. Make sure he is at ease in the tub and have the water at a comfortable temperature. Begin bathing by wetting the coat all the way down to the skin. Massage in the shampoo, keeping it away from his face and eyes. Rinse him thoroughly, again avoiding the eyes and ears, as you don't want to get water into the ear canals. A thorough rinsing is important, as shampoo residue is drying and itchy to the dog. After rinsing, wrap him in a towel to absorb the initial moisture, and then finish the job with a fresh dry towel. You should keep the dog indoors and away from drafts until he is completely dry.

Nail Clipping

Having his nails trimmed is not on many dogs' lists of favorite things to do. With this in mind, you will need to accustom your puppy to the procedure at a young age so that he will sit still (well, as still as he can) for his pedicures. Long nails can cause the dog's feet to spread, which is not good for him; likewise, long nails can hurt if they unintentionally scratch, not good for you!

Some dogs' nails are worn down naturally by regular walking on hard surfaces, so the frequency with which you clip depends on

THE EARS KNOW

Examining and cleaning your puppy's ears helps ensure good internal health. The ears are the eyes to the dog's innards! Begin handling your puppy's ears when he's still young so that he doesn't protest every time you lift a flap or touch his ears. Yeast and bacteria are two of the culprits that you can detect by examining the ear. You will notice a strong, often foul, odor, debris, redness or some kind of discharge. All of these point to health problems that can worsen over time. Additionally, you are on the lookout for wax accumulation, ear mites and other tiny bothersome parasites and their even tinier droppings. You may have to pluck hair with tweezers in order to have a better view into the dog's ears, but this is painless if done carefully. Obtain an ear-cleaning formula from your vet or pet-supply shop; healthy ears should be cleaned weekly.

your individual dog. Look at his nails from time to time and clip as needed; a good way to know when it's time for a trim is if you hear your dog clicking as he walks across the floor.

There are several types of nail clippers and even electric nail-grinding tools made for dogs; first we'll discuss using the clipper. To start, have your clipper ready and some doggie treats on hand. You want your pup to view his nail-clipping sessions in a positive light, and what better way to convince him than with food? You may want to enlist the help of an assistant to comfort the pup and offer treats as you concentrate on the clipping itself. The guillotine-type clipper is thought of by many as the easiest type to use; the nail tip is inserted into the opening, and blades on the top and bottom snip it off in one clip.

Start by grasping the pup's paw; a little pressure on the foot pad causes the nail to extend, making it easier to clip. Clip off a little at a time. If you can see the "quick," which is a blood vessel that runs through each nail, you will know how much to trim, as you do not want to cut into the quick. On that note, if you do cut the quick, which will cause bleeding, you can stem the flow of blood with a styptic pencil or other clotting agent. If you mistakenly nip the quick, do not panic or fuss, as this will cause the pup to be afraid. Simply reassure the pup, stop the bleeding and move on to the next nail. Don't be discouraged; you will become a professional canine pedicurist with practice.

You may or may not be able to see the quick, so it's best to just clip off a small bit at a time. If you see a dark dot in the center of the nail, this is the quick and your cue to stop clipping. Tell the puppy he's a "good boy" and offer a piece of treat with each nail. You can also use nail-clipping time to examine the footpads, making sure that they are not dry and cracked and that nothing has become embedded in them.

Clipping your dog's nails is a necessity. The nails may wear down somewhat from walking on hard surfaces, but your American Bulldog still should be acclimated to the procedure at a young age.

The nail grinder, the second choice, is many owners' first choice. Accustoming the puppy to the sound of the grinder and sensation of the buzz presents fewer challenges than the clipper, and there's no chance of cutting through the quick. Use the grinder on a low setting and always talk

SCOOTING HIS BOTTOM

Here's a doggy problem that many owners tend to neglect. If your dog is scooting his rear end around the carpet, he probably is experiencing anal-sac impaction or blockage. The anal sacs are the two grape-sized glands on either side of the dog's vent. The dog cannot empty these glands, which become filled with a foul-smelling material. The dog may attempt to lick the area to relieve the pressure. He may also rub his anus on your walls, furniture or floors.

Don't neglect your dog's rear end during grooming sessions. By squeezing both sides of the anus with a soft cloth, you can express some of the material in the sacs. If the material is pasty and thick, you likely will need the assistance of a veterinarian. Vets know how to express the glands and can show you how to do it correctly without hurting the dog or spraying yourself with the unpleasant liquid.

soothingly to your dog. He won't mind his salon visit, and he'll have nicely polished nails as well.

Eye Care

During grooming sessions, pay extra attention to the condition of your dog's eyes. If the area around the eyes is soiled or if tear staining has occurred, there are various cleaning agents made especially for this purpose. Look at the dog's eyes to make sure no debris has entered; dogs with large eyes and those who spend time outdoors are especially prone to this.

The signs of an eye infection are obvious: mucus, redness, puffiness, scabs or other signs of irritation. If your dog's eyes become infected, the vet will likely prescribe an antibiotic ointment for treatment. If you notice signs of more serious problems, such as opacities in the eye, which usually indicate cataracts, consult the vet at once. Taking time to pay attention to your dog's eyes will alert you in the early stages of any problem so that you can get your dog treatment as soon as possible. You could save your dog's sight!

ID FOR YOUR DOG

You love your American Bulldog and want to keep him safe. Of course you take every precaution to prevent his escaping from the yard or becoming lost or stolen. You have a sturdy high fence and you always keep your dog on lead when out and about in public places. If your dog is not properly identified, however, you are overlooking a major aspect of his safety. We hope to never be in a situation where your dog is missing, but you should practice prevention in the unfortunate case that this happens; identification greatly increases the chances of your dog's being returned to you.

There are several ways to identify your dog. First, the traditional dog tag should be a staple in your dog's wardrobe, attached to his everyday collar. Tags can be made of sturdy plastic and various metals and should include your contact information so that a person who finds the dog can get in touch with you right away to arrange his return. Many people today enjoy the wide range of decorative tags available, so have fun and create a tag to match your dog's personality. Of course, it is important that the tag stays on the collar, so have a secure O-ring attachment; you also can explore the type of tag that slides right onto the collar.

In addition to the ID tag, which every dog should wear even if identified by another method, two other forms of identification have become popular: microchipping and tattooing. In microchipping, a tiny scannable chip is painlessly inserted under the dog's skin. The number is registered to you so that if your lost dog turns up at a clinic or shelter the chip can be scanned to retrieve your contact information.

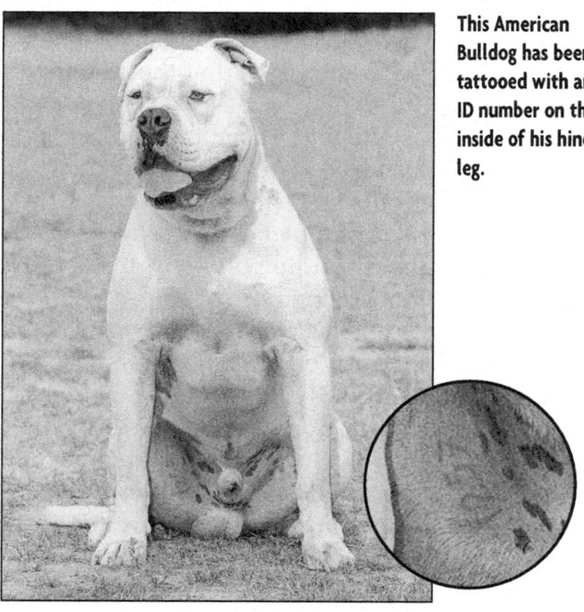

This American Bulldog has been tattooed with an ID number on the inside of his hind leg.

The advantage of the microchip is that it is a permanent form of ID, but there are some factors to consider. Several different companies make microchips, and not all are compatible with the others' scanning devices. It's best to find a company with a universal microchip that can be read by scanners made by other companies as well. It won't do any good to have the dog chipped if the information cannot be retrieved. Also, not every humane society, shelter and clinic is equipped with a scanner, although more and more facilities are equipping

PET OR STRAY?

Besides the obvious benefit of providing your contact information to whoever finds your lost dog, an ID tag makes your dog more approachable and more likely to be recovered. A strange dog wandering the neighborhood without a collar and tags will look like a stray, while the collar and tags indicate that the dog is someone's pet. Even if the ID tags become detached from the collar, the collar alone will make a person more likely to pick up the dog.

themselves. In fact, many shelters microchip dogs that they adopt out to new homes.

Because the microchip is not visible to the eye, the dog must wear a tag that states that he is microchipped so that whoever picks him up will know to have him scanned. He of course also should have a tag with contact information in case his chip cannot be read. Humane societies and veterinary clinics offer micropchipping service, which is usually very affordable.

Though less popular than microchipping, tattooing is another permanent method of ID for dogs. Most vets perform this service, and there are also clinics that perform dog tattooing. This is also an affordable procedure and one that will not cause much discomfort for the dog. It is best to put the tattoo in a visible area, such as the ear or light skin of the inner thigh, to deter theft. It is sad to say that there are cases of dogs' being stolen and sold to research laboratories, but such laboratories will not accept tattooed dogs.

To ensure that the tattoo is effective in aiding your dog's return to you, the tattoo number must be registered with a national organization. That way, when someone finds a tattooed dog, a phone call to the registry will quickly match the dog with his owner.

CAR CAUTION

You may like to bring your canine companion along on the daily errands, but if you will be running in and out from place to place and can't bring him indoors with you, leave him at home. Your dog should never be left alone in the car, not even for a minute—never! A car heats up very quickly, and even a cracked-open window will not help. In fact, leaving the window cracked will be dangerous if the dog tries to escape; it may even attract dog thieves. When in doubt, leave your dog home, where you know he will be safe.

Proper identification tags are the simplest form of ID and should be worn even if your dog is identified by another method.

Training Your

AMERICAN BULLDOG

BASIC TRAINING PRINCIPLES: PUPPY VS. ADULT

There's a big difference between training an adult dog and training a young puppy. With a young puppy, everything is new! At eight to ten weeks of age, he will be experiencing many things, and he has nothing with which to compare these experiences. Up to this point, he has been with his dam and littermates, not one-on-one with people except in his interactions with his breeder and visitors to the litter.

When you first bring the puppy home, he is eager to please you. This means that he accepts doing things your way. During the next couple of months, he will absorb the basis of everything he needs to know for the rest of his life. This early age is even referred to as the "sponge" stage. After that, for the next 18 months, it's up to you to reinforce good manners by building on the foundation that you've established. Once your puppy is reliable in basic commands and behavior and has reached the appropriate age, you may gradually introduce him to some of the interesting sports, games and activities available to pet owners and their dogs.

Raising your puppy is a family affair. Each member of the family must know what rules to set forth for the puppy and how to use the same one-word commands to mean exactly the same thing every time. Even if yours is a large family, one person will soon be considered by the pup to be the leader, the Alpha person in his pack, the "boss" who must be obeyed. Often that highly regarded person turns out to be the one

Take advantage of your youngster's ability to learn. Get started with simple lessons when he first comes home with you.

An American Bulldog makes a bright, inquisitive student, eager to please the pack leader he respects.

who feeds the puppy. Food ranks very high on the puppy's list of important things! That's why your puppy is rewarded with small treats along with verbal praise when he responds to you correctly. As the puppy learns to do what you want him to do, the food rewards are gradually eliminated and only the praise remains. If you were to keep up with the food treats, you could have two problems on your hands—an obese dog and a beggar.

Training begins the minute your American Bulldog puppy steps through the doorway of your home, so don't make the mistake of putting the puppy on the floor and telling him by your actions to "Go for it! Run wild!" Even if this is your first puppy, you must act as if you know what you're doing: be the boss. An uncertain pup may be terrified to move, while a bold one will be ready to take you at your word and start plotting to destroy the house! Before you collected your puppy, you decided where his own special place would be, and that's where to put him when you first arrive home. Give him a house tour after he has investigated his area and had a nap and a bathroom "pit stop."

It's worth mentioning here that, if you've adopted an adult dog that is completely trained to your liking, lucky you! You're off the hook! However, if that dog spent his life up to this point in a kennel, or even in a good home but without any real training, be prepared to tackle the job ahead. A dog three years of age or older with no previous training cannot be blamed for not knowing what he was never taught. While the

"SCHOOL" MODE

When is your puppy ready for a lesson? Maybe not always when you are. Attempting training with treats just before his mealtime is asking for disaster. Notice what times of day he performs best and make that Fido's school time.

dog is trying to understand and learn your rules, at the same time he has to unlearn many of his previously self-taught habits and general view of the world.

Working with a professional trainer will speed up your progress with an adopted adult dog. You'll need patience, too. Some new rules may be close to impossible for the dog to accept. After all, he's been successful so far by doing everything his way! (Patience again.) He may agree with your instruction for a few days and then slip back into his old ways, so you must be just as consistent and understanding in your teaching as you would be with a puppy. (More patience needed yet again!) Your dog has to learn to pay attention to your voice, your family, the daily routine, new smells, new sounds and, in some cases, even a new climate.

One of the most important things to find out about a newly adopted adult dog is his reaction to children (yours and others), strangers and your friends, and how he acts upon meeting other dogs. If he was not socialized with dogs as a puppy, this could be a major problem. This does not mean that he's a "bad" dog, or a vicious dog; rather, it means that he has no idea how to read another dog's body language. There's no way for him to tell whether the other dog is a friend

BE UPSTANDING!
You are the dog's leader. During training, stand up straight so your dog looks up at you, and therefore up *to* you. Say the command words distinctly, in a clear, declarative tone of voice. (No barking!) Give rewards only as the correct response takes place (remember your timing!). Praise, smiles and treats are "rewards" used to positively reinforce correct responses. Don't repeat a mistake. Just change to another exercise—you will soon find success!

or foe. Survival instinct takes over, telling him to attack first and ask questions later. This definitely calls for professional help and, even then, may not be a behavior that can be corrected 100% reliably (or even at all). Socialization is *so* important in the American Bulldog and something that cannot be overlooked with any breed. If you have a puppy, this is why it is so very important to introduce your young puppy properly to other puppies and "dog-friendly" adult dogs.

DAILY SCHEDULE

How many relief trips does your puppy need per day? A puppy up to the age of 14 weeks will need to go outside about 8 to 12 times per day! You will have to take the pup out any time he starts sniffing around the floor or turning in small circles, as well as after naps, meals, games and lessons or whenever he's released from his crate. Once the puppy is 14 to 22 weeks of age, he will require only 6 to 8 relief trips. At the ages of 22 to 32 weeks, the puppy will require about 5 to 7 trips. Adult dogs typically require 4 relief trips per day, in the morning, afternoon, evening and late at night.

HOUSE-TRAINING YOUR AMERICAN BULLDOG

Dogs are tactility-oriented when it comes to house-training. In other words, they respond to the surface on which they are given approval to eliminate. The choice is yours (the dog's version is in parentheses): The lawn (including the neighbors' lawns)? A bare patch of earth under a tree (where people like to sit and relax in the summertime)? Concrete steps or patio (all sidewalks, garages and basement floors)? The curbside (watch out for cars)? A small area of crushed stone in a corner of the yard (mine!)? The latter is the best choice if you can manage it, because it will remain strictly for the dog's use and is easy to keep clean.

House-training your dog includes location training. Decide on the area in which you want your dog to relieve himself before he chooses a spot on his own.

You can start out with paper-training indoors and switch over to an outdoor surface as the puppy matures and gains control

Canine Development Schedule

It is important to understand how and at what age a puppy develops into adulthood. If you are a puppy owner, consult this Canine Development Schedule to determine the stage of development your puppy is currently experiencing. This knowledge will help you as you work with the puppy in the weeks and months ahead.

Period	Age	Characteristics
First to Third	Birth to Seven Weeks	Puppy needs food, sleep and warmth and responds to simple and gentle touching. Needs mother for security and disciplining. Needs littermates for learning and interacting with other dogs. Pup learns to function within a pack and learns pack order of dominance. Begin socializing pup with adults and children for short periods. Pup begins to become aware of his environment.
Fourth	Eight to Twelve Weeks	Brain is fully developed. Pup needs socializing with outside world. Remove from mother and littermates. Needs to change from canine pack to human pack. Human dominance necessary. Fear period occurs between 8 and 12 weeks. Avoid fright and pain.
Fifth	Thirteen to Sixteen Weeks	Training and formal obedience should begin. Less association with other dogs, more with people, places, situations. Period will pass easily if you remember this is pup's change-to-adolescence time. Be firm and fair. Flight instinct prominent. Permissiveness and overdisciplining can do permanent damage. Praise for good behavior.
Juvenile	Four to Eight Months	Another fear period at about 7 to 8 months of age. It passes quickly, but be cautious of fright and pain. Sexual maturity reached. Dominant traits established. Dog should understand sit, down, come and stay by now.

Note: These are approximate time frames. Allow for individual differences in puppies.

over his need to eliminate. For the nay-sayers, don't worry—this won't mean that the dog will soil on every piece of newspaper lying around the house. You are training him to go outside, remember? Starting out by paper-training often is the only choice for a city dog.

When Your Puppy's "Got to Go"
Your puppy's need to relieve himself is seemingly non-stop, but signs of improvement will be seen each week. From 8 to 10 weeks old, the puppy will have to be taken outside every time he wakes up, about 10–15 minutes after every meal and after every period of play—all day long, from first thing in the morning until his bedtime! That's a total of ten or more trips per day to teach the puppy where it's okay to relieve himself. With that schedule in mind, you can see that house-training a young puppy is not a part-time job. It requires someone to be home all day.

If that seems overwhelming or impossible, do a little planning. For example, plan to pick up your puppy at the start of a vacation period. If you can't get home in the middle of the day, plan to hire a dog-sitter or ask a neighbor to come over to take the pup outside, feed him his lunch and then take him out again about ten or so minutes

EXTRA! EXTRA!
The headlines read: "Puppy Piddles Here!" Breeders commonly use newspapers to line their whelping pens, so puppies learn to associate newspapers with relieving themselves. Do not use newspapers to line your pup's crate, as this will signal to your puppy that it is OK to urinate in his crate. If you choose to paper-train your puppy, you will layer newspapers on a section of the floor near the door he uses to go outside. You should encourage the puppy to use the papers to relieve himself, and bring him there whenever you see him getting ready to go. Little by little, you will reduce the size of the newspaper-covered area so that the puppy will learn to relieve himself "on the other side of the door."

after he's eaten. Also make arrangements with that or another person to be your "emergency" contact if you have to stay late on the job. Remind yourself—repeatedly—that this hectic schedule improves as the puppy gets older.

Home within a Home

Your American Bulldog puppy needs to be confined to one secure, puppy-proof area when no one is able to watch his every move. Generally, the kitchen is the place of choice because the floor is washable. Likewise, it's a busy family area that will accustom the pup to a variety of noises, everything from pots and pans to the telephone, blender and dishwasher. He will also be enchanted by the smell of your cooking (and will never be critical when you burn something). An exercise pen (also called an "ex-pen," a puppy version of a playpen) within the room of choice is an excellent means of confinement for a young pup. He can see out and has a certain amount of space in which to run about, but he is safe from dangerous things like electrical cords, heating units, trash baskets or open kitchen-supply cabinets. Place the pen where the puppy will not get a blast of heat or air conditioning.

In the pen, you can put a few toys, his bed (which can be his crate if the dimensions of pen and crate are compatible) and a few layers of newspaper in one small corner, just in case. A water bowl can be hung at a convenient height on the side of the ex-pen so it won't become a splashing pool for an innovative puppy. His food dish can go on the floor, next to the water bowl.

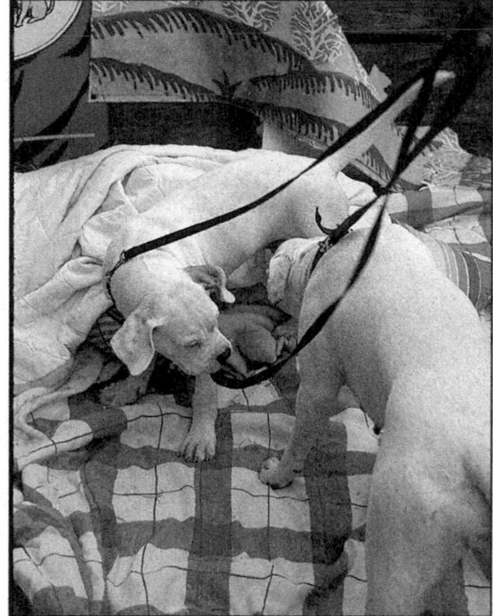

Puppies are curious and like to investigate new things. Part of "control" is making sure that your pup's curiosity does not get him into trouble.

Crates are something that pet owners are at last getting used to for their dogs. Wild or domestic canines have always preferred to sleep in denlike safe spots, and that is exactly what the crate provides. How often have you seen adult dogs that choose to sleep under a table or chair even though they have full run of the house? It's the den connection.

In your "happy" voice, use the word "Crate" every time you

> **SOMEBODY TO BLAME**
> House-training a puppy can be frustrating for the puppy and the owner alike. The puppy does not instinctively understand the difference between defecating on the pavement outside and on the ceramic tile in the kitchen. He is confused and frightened by his human's exuberant reactions to his natural urges. The owner, arguably the more intelligent of the duo, is also frustrated that he cannot convince his puppy to obey his commands and instructions.
>
> In frustration, the owner may struggle with the temptation to discipline the puppy, scold him or even strike him on the rear end. These harsh corrections are unnecessary and inappropriate, serving to defeat your purpose in gaining your puppy's trust and respect. Don't blame your nine-week-old puppy. Blame yourself for not being 100% consistent in the puppy's lessons and routine. The lesson here is simple: try harder and your puppy will succeed.

put the pup into his den. If he's new to a crate, toss in a small biscuit for him to chase the first few times. At night, after he's been outside, he should sleep in his crate. The crate may be kept in his designated area at night or, if you want to be sure to hear those wake-up yips in the morning, put the crate in a corner of your bedroom. However, don't make any response whatsoever to whining or crying. If he's completely ignored, he'll settle down and get to sleep.

Good bedding for a young puppy is an old folded bath towel or an old blanket, something that is easily washable and disposable if necessary ("accidents" will happen!). Never put newspaper in the puppy's crate. Also, those old ideas about adding a clock to replace his mother's heartbeat, or a hot-water bottle to replace her warmth, are just that—old ideas. The clock could drive the puppy nuts, and the hot-water bottle could end up as a very soggy waterbed! An extremely good breeder would have introduced your puppy to the crate by letting two pups sleep together for a couple of nights, followed by several nights alone. How thankful you will be if you found that breeder!

Safe toys in the pup's crate or area will keep him occupied, but monitor their condition closely. Discard any toys that show signs of being chewed to bits. Squeaky parts, bits of stuffing or plastic or any other small pieces can cause intestinal blockage or possibly choking if swallowed.

Progressing with Potty-Training

After you've taken your puppy out and he has relieved himself in the area you've selected, he can have some free time with the family as long as there is someone responsible for watching him. That doesn't mean just someone in the same room who is watching TV or busy on the computer, but one person who is doing nothing other than keeping an eye on the pup, playing with him on the floor and helping him understand his position in the pack.

This first taste of freedom will let you begin to set the house rules. If you don't want the dog on the furniture, now is the time to prevent his first attempts to jump up onto the couch. The word to use in this case is "Off," not "Down." "Down" is the word you will use to teach the down position, which is something entirely different.

Most corrections at this stage come in the form of simply distracting the puppy. Instead of telling him "No" for "Don't chew the carpet," distract the chomping puppy with a toy and he'll forget about the carpet.

LEASH TRAINING

House-training and leash training go hand in hand, literally. When taking your puppy outside to do his business, lead him there on his leash. Unless an emergency potty run is called for, do not whisk the puppy up into your arms and take him outside. If you have a fenced yard, you have the advantage of letting the puppy loose to go out, but it's better to put the dog on the leash and take him to his designated place in the yard until he is reliably house-trained. Taking the puppy for a walk is the best way to house-train a dog. The dog will associate the walk with his time to relieve himself, and the exercise of walking stimulates the dog's bowels and bladder. Dogs that are not trained to relieve themselves on a walk may hold it until they get back home, which of course defeats half the purpose of the walk.

As you are playing with the pup, do not forget to watch him closely and pay attention to his body language. Whenever you see him begin to circle or sniff, take the puppy outside to relieve himself. If you are paper-training, put him back into his confined area on the newspapers. In either case, praise him as he eliminates while he actually is in the act of relieving himself. Three seconds after he has finished is too late! You'll be praising him for running toward you, picking up

Male dogs like to leave their urinary "calling cards" on upright objects like fence posts, trash cans, trees, etc.

a toy or whatever he may be doing at that moment, and that's not what you want to be praising him for. Timing is a vital tool in all dog training. Use it!

Remove soiled newspapers immediately and replace them with clean ones. You may want to take a small piece of soiled paper and place it in the middle of the new clean papers, as the scent will attract him to that spot when it's time to go again. That scent attraction is why it's so important to clean up any messes made in the house by using a product specially made to eliminate the odor of dog urine and droppings. Regular household cleansers won't do the trick. Pet shops sell the best pet deodorizers. Invest in the largest container—you will use it!

Scent attraction eventually will lead your pup to his chosen spot outdoors; this is the basis of outdoor training. When you take your puppy outside to relieve himself, use a one-word command such as "Outside" or "Go-potty" (that's one word to the puppy!) as you pick him up and attach his leash. Then put him down in his area. If you cannot carry him, snap the leash on quickly and lead him to his spot. Now comes the hard part—hard for you, that is. Just stand there until he urinates and defecates. Move him a few feet in one direction or another if he's just sitting there looking at you, but remember that this is neither playtime nor time for a walk. This is strictly a business trip! Then, as he circles and squats (remember your timing!), give him a quiet "Good dog" as praise. If you start to jump for joy, ecstatic over his performance, he'll do one of two things: either he will stop midstream, as it were, or he'll do it again for you—in the house—and expect you to be just as delighted!

Give him five minutes or so and, if he doesn't go in that time, take him back indoors to his confined area and try again in another ten minutes, or immediately if you see him sniffing and circling. By careful observation, you'll soon work out a successful schedule.

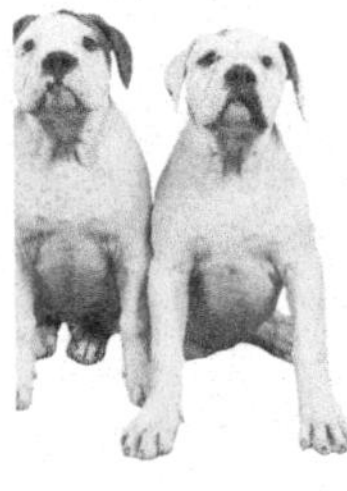

BASIC PRINCIPLES OF DOG TRAINING

1. Start training early. A young puppy is ready, willing and able.
2. Timing is your all-important tool. Praise at the exact time that the dog responds correctly. Pay close attention.
3. Patience is almost as important as timing!
4. Repeat! The same word has to mean the same thing every time.
5. In the beginning, praise all correct behavior verbally, along with treats and petting.

Accidents, by the way, are just that—accidents. Clean them up quickly and thoroughly, without comment, after the puppy has been taken outside to finish his business and then put back into his area or crate. If you witness an accident in progress, say "No!" in a stern voice and get the pup outdoors immediately. No punishment is needed. You and your puppy are just learning each other's language, and sometimes it's easy to miss a puppy's message. Chalk it up to experience and watch more closely from now on.

KEEPING THE PACK ORDERLY

Discipline is a form of training that brings order to life. For example, military discipline is what allows the soldiers in an army to work as one. Discipline is a form of teaching and, in dogs, is the basis of how the successful pack operates. Each member knows his place in the pack and all respect the leader, or Alpha dog. It is essential for your puppy that you establish this type of relationship, with you as the Alpha, or leader. It is a form of social coexistence that all canines recognize and accept. Discipline, therefore, is never to be confused with punishment. When you teach your puppy how you want him to behave, and he behaves properly and you praise him for it, you are disciplining him with a form of positive reinforcement.

WHO'S TRAINING WHOM?

Dog training is a black-and-white exercise. The correct response to a command must be absolute, and the trainer must insist on completely accurate responses from the dog. A trainer cannot command his dog to sit and then settle for the dog's melting into the down position. Often owners are so pleased that their dogs "did something" in response to a command that they just shrug and say, "OK, down" even though they wanted the dog to sit. You want your dog to respond to the command without hesitation: he must respond at that moment and correctly every time.

For a dog, rewards come in the form of praise, a smile, a

Don't be "all work and no play." Puppies have short attention spans and need time for fun in between lessons if you hope to keep their interest.

cheerful tone of voice, a few friendly pats or a rub of the ears. Rewards are also small food treats. Obviously, that does not mean bits of regular dog food. Instead, treats are very small bits of special things like cheese or pieces of soft dog treats. The idea is to reward the dog with something very small that he can taste and swallow, providing instant positive reinforcement. If he has to take time to chew the treat, he will have forgotten what he did to earn it by the time he is finished!

Your puppy should never be physically punished. The displeasure shown on your face and in your voice is sufficient to signal to the pup that he has done something wrong. He wants to please everyone higher up on the social ladder, especially his leader, so a scowl and harsh voice will take care of the error. Growling out the word "Shame!" when the pup is caught in the act of doing something wrong is better than the repetitive "No." Some dogs hear "No" so often that they begin to think it's their name! By the way, do not use the dog's name when you're correcting him. His name is reserved to get his attention for something pleasant about to take place.

There are punishments that have nothing to do with you. For example, your dog may think that chasing cats is one reason for his existence. You can try to stop it as much as you like but without success, because it's such fun for the dog. But one good hissing, spitting swipe of a cat's claws across the dog's nose will put an end to the game forever. Intervene only when your dog's eyeball is seriously at risk. Cat scratches can cause

SMILE WHEN YOU ORDER ME AROUND!

While trainers recommend practicing with your dog every day, it's perfectly acceptable to take a "mental health day" off. It's better not to train the dog on days when you're in a sour mood. Your bad attitude or lack of interest will be sensed by your dog, and he will respond accordingly. Studies show that dogs are well-tuned-in to their humans' emotions. Be conscious of how you use your voice when talking to your dog. Raising your voice or shouting will only erode your dog's trust in you as his trainer and master.

permanent damage to an innocent but annoying puppy.

PUPPY KINDERGARTEN

Collar and Leash

Before you begin your American Bulldog puppy's education, he must be used to his collar and leash. Choose a collar for your puppy that is secure, but not heavy or bulky. He won't enjoy training if he's uncomfortable. A flat buckle collar is fine for everyday wear and for initial puppy training. For older dogs, there are several types of training collars such as the martingale, which is a double loop that tightens slightly around the neck, or the head collar, which is similar to a horse's halter. Do not use a chain choke collar unless you have been specifically shown how to put it on and how to use it correctly. You may not be disposed to use a chain choke collar even if your breeder has told you that it's suitable for your American Bulldog. In fact, any type of training collar will be ineffective and also can injure a dog if used improperly.

A lightweight 6-foot woven cotton or nylon training leash is preferred by most trainers because it is easy to fold up in your hand and comfortable to hold because there is a certain amount of give to it. There are lessons where the dog will start off 6 feet away from you at the end of the leash. The leash used to take the puppy outside to relieve himself is shorter because you don't want him to roam away from his area. The shorter leash will also be the one to use when you walk the puppy.

If you've been wise enough to enroll in a Puppy Kindergarten training class, suggestions will be made as to the best collar and leash for your young puppy. I say "wise" because your puppy will be in a class with puppies in his age range (up to five months old)

Before any training can begin, you must have a sturdy collar and lead that your Bulldog is accustomed to wearing.

A dog treat or a small piece of food, like cheese or cooked chicken, is an excellent training incentive.

of all breeds and sizes. It's the perfect way for him to learn the right way (and the wrong way) to interact with other dogs as well as their people. You cannot teach your puppy how to interpret another dog's sign language. For a first-time puppy owner, these socialization classes are invaluable. For experienced dog owners, they are a real boon to further training.

Begin and end every training exercise on a high note by doing a successful sit or something else the dog knows well.

Attention

You've been using the dog's name since the minute you collected him from the breeder, so you should be able to get his attention by saying his name—with a big smile and in an excited tone of voice. His response will be the puppy equivalent of "Here I am! What are we going to do?" Your immediate response (if you haven't guessed by now) is "Good dog." Rewarding him at the moment he pays attention to you teaches him the proper way to respond when he hears his name.

EXERCISES FOR A BASIC CANINE EDUCATION

The Sit Exercise

There are several ways to teach the puppy to sit. The first one is to catch him whenever he is about to sit and, as his backside nears the floor, say "Sit, good dog!" That's positive reinforcement and, if your timing is sharp, he will learn that what he's doing at that second is connected to your saying "Sit" and that you think he's clever for doing it!

Another method is to start with the puppy on his leash in front of you. Show him a treat in the palm of your right hand. Bring your hand up under his nose and, almost in slow motion, move your hand up and back so his nose goes up in the air and his head tilts back as he follows the treat in your hand. At that point, he will have to either sit or fall over, so as his back legs buckle under, say "Sit, good dog," and then give him the treat and lots of praise. You may have to begin with your hand lightly running up his chest, actually lifting his chin up until he sits. Some (usually older) dogs require gentle pressure on their hindquarters with the left hand, in which case the dog should be on your left side. Puppies generally do not appreciate this physical dominance.

After a few times, you should be able to show the dog a treat in the open palm of your hand, raise your hand waist-high as you say "Sit" and have him sit. Once again, you have taught him two things at the same time. Both the verbal command and the motion of the hand are signals for the sit. Your puppy is watching you almost more than he is listening to you, so what you do is just as important as what you say.

Don't save any of these drills only for training sessions. Use them as much as possible at odd times during a normal day. The dog should always sit before being given his food dish. He should sit to let you go through a doorway first, when the doorbell rings or when you stop to speak to someone on the street.

Down is an important exercise that must be taught properly, with attention to how the dog regards the exercise.

The Down Exercise

Before beginning to teach the down command, you must consider how the dog feels about this exercise. To him, "Down" is a submissive position. Being flat on the floor with you standing over him is not his idea of fun. It's up to you to let him know that, while it may not be fun, the reward of your approval is worth his effort.

Start with the puppy on your left side in a sit position. Hold the leash right above his collar in your left hand. Have an extra-special treat, such as a small piece of cooked chicken or hot dog, in your right hand. Place it at the end of the pup's nose and steadily move your hand down and forward along the ground. Hold the leash to prevent a sudden lunge for the food. As the puppy goes into the down position, say "Down" very gently.

The difficulty with this exercise is twofold: it's both the submissive aspect and the fact that most people say the word "Down" as if they were a drill sergeant in charge of recruits! So issue the command sweetly, give him the treat and have the pup maintain the down position for several seconds. If he tries to get up immediately, place your hands on his shoulders and press down gently, giving him a very quiet "Good dog." As you progress with this lesson, increase the "down time" until he will hold it until you say "Okay" (his cue for release). Practice this one in the house at various times throughout the day.

By increasing the length of time during which the dog must maintain the down position, you'll find many uses for it. For example, he can lie at your feet in the vet's office or anywhere that both of you have to wait, when you are on the phone, while the family is eating and so forth. If you progress to training for competitive obedience, he'll already be all set for the exercise called the "long down."

TRAINING AND SAFETY

1. Whether on- or off-leash, practice only in a fenced area.
2. Remove the training collar when the training session is over.
3. Don't try to break up a dog-fight.
4. "Come," "Leave it" and "Wait" are safety commands.
5. The dog belongs in a crate or behind a barrier when riding in the car.
6. Don't ignore the dog's first sign of aggression. Aggression only gets worse, so take it seriously.
7. Keep the faces of children and dogs separated.
8. Pay attention to what the dog is chewing.
9. Keep the vet's number near your phone.
10. "Okay" is a useful release command.

THE STAY EXERCISE

You can teach your American Bulldog to stay in the sit, down and stand positions. To teach the sit/stay, have the dog sit on your left side. Hold the leash at waist level in your left hand and let the dog know that you have a treat in your closed right hand. Step forward on your right foot as you say "Stay." Immediately turn and stand directly in front of the dog, keeping your right hand up high so he'll keep his eye on the treat hand and maintain the sit position for a count of five. Return to your original position and offer the reward.

Increase the length of the sit/stay each time until the dog can hold it for at least 30 seconds without moving. After about a week of success, move out on your right foot and take two steps before turning to face the dog. Give the "Stay" hand signal (left palm back toward the dog's head) as you leave. He gets the treat when you return and he holds the sit/stay. Increase the distance that you walk away from him before turning until you reach the length of your training leash. But don't rush it! Go back to the beginning if he moves before he should. No matter what the lesson, never be upset by having to back up for a few days. The repetition and practice are what will make your dog reliable in these commands. It won't do any good to move on to something more difficult if the command is not mastered at the easier levels. Above all, even if you do get frustrated, never let your puppy know! Always keep a positive, upbeat attitude during training, which will transmit to your dog for positive results.

The down/stay is taught in the same way once the dog is completely reliable and steady with the down command. Again, don't rush it. With the dog in the down position on your left side, step out on your right foot as you say "Stay." Return by walking around in back of the dog and into your original position. While you are training, it's okay to murmur something like "Hold on" to encourage him to stay put. When the dog will stay without moving when you are at a distance of 3 or 4 feet, begin to increase the length of time before you return. Be sure he holds the down on your return until you say "Okay." At that point, he gets his treat—just so he'll remember for next time that it's not over until it's over.

The Come Exercise

No command is more important to the safety of your American Bulldog than "Come." It is what you should say every single time you see the puppy running toward you: "Binky, come! Good dog." During playtime, run a few feet away from the puppy and turn and tell him to "Come" as he is already running to you. You can go so far as to teach your puppy two things at once if you squat down and hold out your arms. As the pup gets close to

You want your American Bulldog to come to you every time you call him.

Teaching the heel is very important, or else you may end up with a dog who tries to take *you* for a walk.

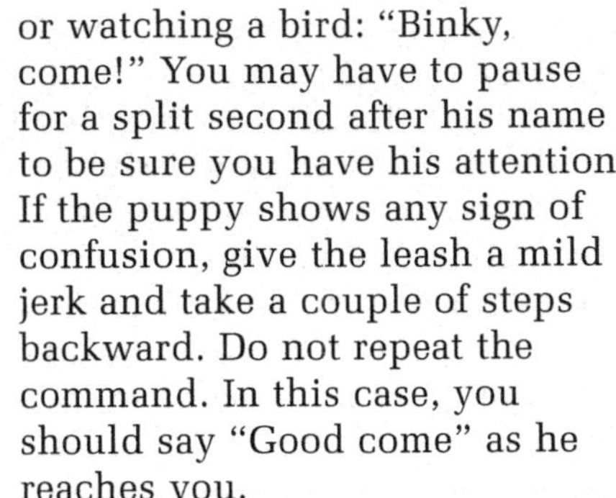

you and you're saying "Good dog," bring your right arm in about waist high. Now he's also learning the hand signal, an excellent device should you be on the phone when you need to get him to come to you! You'll also both be one step ahead when you enter obedience classes.

When the puppy responds to your well-timed "Come," try it with the puppy on the training leash. This time, catch him off guard, while he's sniffing a leaf or watching a bird: "Binky, come!" You may have to pause for a split second after his name to be sure you have his attention. If the puppy shows any sign of confusion, give the leash a mild jerk and take a couple of steps backward. Do not repeat the command. In this case, you should say "Good come" as he reaches you.

That's the number-one rule of training. Each command word is given just once. Anything more is nagging. You'll also notice that all commands are one word only. Even when they are actually two words, you say them as one.

Never call the dog to come to you—with or without his name—if you are angry or intend to correct him for some misbehavior. When correcting the pup, you go to him. Your dog must always connect "Come" with something pleasant and with your approval; then you can rely on his response.

Puppies, like children, have notoriously short attention spans, so don't overdo it with any of the training. Keep each lesson short. Break it up with a quick run around the yard or a ball toss, repeat the lesson and quit as soon as the pup gets it right. That way, you will always end with a "Good dog."

Life isn't perfect and neither are puppies. A time will come, often around ten months of age,

THE BEST INVESTMENT

Obedience school is as important for you and your dog as grammar school is for your kids, and it's a lot more fun! Don't shun classes, thinking that your dog might embarrass you. He might! Instructors don't expect you to know everything, but they'll teach you the correct way to teach your dog so he won't embarrass you again. He'll become a social animal as you learn with other people and dogs. Home training, while effective in teaching your dog the basic commands, excludes these socialization benefits.

when he'll become "selectively deaf" or choose to "forget" his name. He may respond by wagging his tail (and even seeming to smile at you) with a look that says "Make me!" Laugh, throw his favorite toy and skip the lesson you had planned. Pups will be pups!

The Heel Exercise

The second-most important command to teach, after the come, is the heel. When you are walking your growing puppy, you need to be in control. Besides, it looks terrible to be pulled and yanked down the street, and it's not much fun either. Your eight- to ten-week-old puppy will probably follow you everywhere, but that's his natural instinct, not your control over the situation. However, any time he does follow you, you can say "Heel" and be ahead of the game, as he will learn to associate this command with the action of following you before you even begin teaching him to heel.

There is a very precise, almost military, procedure for teaching your dog to heel. As with all other obedience training, begin with the dog on your left side. He will be in a very nice sit and you will have the training leash across your chest. Hold the loop and folded leash in your right hand. Pick up the slack leash above the dog in your left hand and hold it loosely at your side. Step out on your left foot as you say "Heel." If the puppy does not move, give a gentle tug or pat your left leg to get him started. If he surges ahead of you, stop and pull him back gently until he is at your side. Tell him to sit and begin again.

Walk a few steps and stop while the puppy is correctly beside you. Tell him to sit and give mild verbal praise. (More enthusiastic praise will encourage him to think the lesson is over.) Repeat the lesson, increasing the number of steps you take only as long as the dog is heeling nicely beside you.

Sitting by your side is the proper position from which your American Bulldog should start the heel.

Up and over! If you did not see it, you would not believe it. The agility of an American Bulldog is astounding.

When you end the lesson, have him hold the sit, then give him the "Okay" to let him know that this is the end of the lesson. Praise him so that he knows he did a good job.

NO MORE TREATS!

When your dog is responding promptly and correctly to commands, it's time to eliminate treats. Begin by alternating a treat reward with a verbal-praise-only reward. Gradually eliminate all treats while increasing the frequency of praise. Overlook pleading eyes and expectant expressions, but if he's still watching your treat hand, you're on your way to using hand signals.

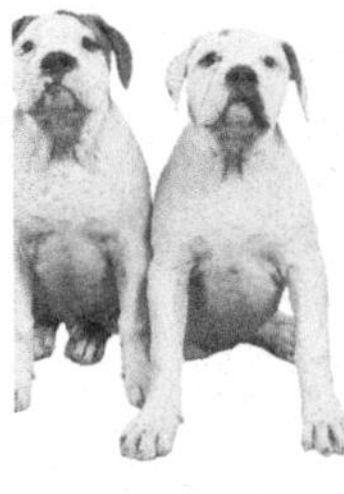

The cure for excessive pulling (a common problem) is to stop when the dog is no more than 2 or 3 feet ahead of you. Guide him back into position and begin again. With a really determined puller, try switching to a head collar. When used correctly, this will automatically turn the pup's head toward you so you can bring him back easily to the heel position. Give quiet, reassuring praise every time the leash goes slack and he's staying with you.

Staying and heeling can take a lot out of a dog, so provide playtime and free-running exercise to shake off the stress when the lessons are over. You don't want him to associate training with all work and no fun.

TRAINING FOR OTHER ACTIVITIES

Once your dog has basic obedience under his collar and is 12 months of age, you can enter the world of competitive dog sport. Obedience trials demonstrate the dog's knowledge of basic commands and progress to very challenging levels. Agility competition is pure fun, like being turned loose in an amusement park full of obstacles! In addition to obedience and agility, in which all breeds can participate, there are some other types of competition that are very well suited for American Bulldogs and similar breeds. Weight-pulling is an exciting event for strong dogs, and many bully breeds participate. The United Kennel Club (UKC) offers obedience, agility and weight-pulling for the American Bulldog. Schutzhund is a form of protection-work training, but it must be done with a reputable, experienced trainer to develop your American Bulldog's protective instincts properly and controllably. Tracking is a sport open to all breeds with a nose—so that means all breeds! For those who like to volunteer, there is the wonderful feeling of owning a therapy dog and visiting hospices, nursing homes and veterans' homes to bring smiles, comfort and companionship to those who live there.

The handsome American Bulldog in show pose is certainly an impressive sight.

Around the house, your American Bulldog can be taught to do some simple chores. You might teach him to carry a basket of household items or to fetch the morning newspaper. The kids can teach the dog all kinds of tricks, from playing hide-and-seek to balancing a biscuit on his nose. A family dog is what rounds out the family. Everything he does, including sitting in your lap and gazing lovingly at you, represents the bonus of owning a dog.

Guiding over the agility see-saw. To learn how to navigate the agility obstacles, a dog needs an able copilot.

Starting out with a well-bred puppy from a reputable breeder gives you the best odds of having a healthy, long-lived companion.

Health Care of Your
AMERICAN BULLDOG

HEALTHCARE FOR A LIFETIME

When you own a dog, you become his healthcare advocate over his entire lifespan, as well as being the one to shoulder the financial burden of such care. Accordingly, it is worthwhile to focus on prevention rather than treatment, as you and your pet will both be happier.

Of course, the best place to have begun your program of preventive healthcare is with the initial purchase or adoption of your dog. There is no way of guaranteeing that your new furry friend is free of medical problems, but there are some things you can do to improve your odds. You certainly should have done adequate research into the American Bulldog and have selected your puppy carefully rather than buying on impulse. Health issues aside, a large number of pet abandonment and relinquishment cases arise from a mismatch between pet needs and owner expectations. This is entirely preventable with appropriate planning and finding a good breeder.

Regarding healthcare issues specifically, it is very difficult to make blanket statements about where to acquire a problem-free pet, but, again, a reputable breeder is your best bet. In an ideal situation, you have the opportunity to see both parents, get references from other owners of the breeder's pups and see genetic-testing documentation for several generations of the litter's ancestors. At the very least, you must thoroughly investigate the American Bulldog and the problems inherent in that breed, as well as the genetic testing available to screen for those problems. Genetic testing offers some important benefits, but testing is available for only a few disorders in a relatively small number of breeds and is not available for some of the most common genetic diseases, such as hip dysplasia, cataracts, epilepsy, cardiomyopathy, etc. This area of research is indeed exciting and increasingly important, and advances will continue to be made each year. In fact, recent research has shown that there is an equivalent dog gene for 75% of known human genes, so research done in either species is likely to benefit the other.

We've also discussed that evaluating the behavioral nature of your American Bulldog and that of his immediate family members is an important part of the selection process that cannot be underestimated or overemphasized. It is sometimes difficult to evaluate temperament in puppies, because certain behavioral tendencies, such as some forms of aggression, may not be immediately evident. More dogs are euthanized each year for behavioral reasons than for all medical conditions combined, so it is critical to take temperament issues seriously. Start with a well-balanced, friendly companion and put the time and effort into proper socialization, and you will both be rewarded with a lifelong valued relationship.

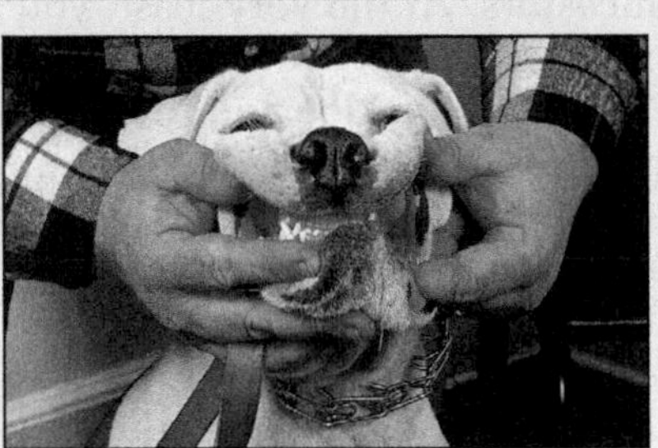

DOGGIE DENTAL DON'TS

A veterinary dental exam is necessary if you notice one or any combination of the following in your dog:

- Broken, loose or missing teeth
- Loss of appetite (which could be due to mouth pain or illness caused by infection)
- Gum abnormalities, including redness, swelling and bleeding
- Drooling, with or without blood
- Yellowing of the teeth or gum line, indicating tartar
- Bad breath

Assuming that you have started off with a pup from healthy, sound stock, you then become responsible for helping your veterinarian keep your pet healthy. Some crucial things happen before you even bring your puppy home. Parasite control typically begins at two weeks of age, and vaccinations typically begin at six to eight weeks of age. A pre-pubertal evaluation is typically scheduled for about six months of age. At this time, a dental evaluation is done (since the adult teeth are now in), heartworm prevention is started and neutering or spaying is most commonly done.

It is critical to commence regular dental care at home if you have not already done so. It may not sound very important, but most dogs have active periodontal disease by four years of age if they don't have their teeth cleaned regularly at home, not just at their veterinary exams. Dental problems lead to more than just bad "doggie breath." Gum disease can have very serious medical consequences. If you start brushing your dog's teeth and using antiseptic rinses from a young age, your dog will be accustomed to it and will not resist. The results will be healthy dentition, which your pet will need to enjoy a long, healthy life.

Most dogs are considered adults at around a year of age, although the American Bulldog continues maturing physically until two to three years of age. Even individual dogs within each breed have different healthcare requirements, so work with your veterinarian to determine what will be needed and what your role should be. This doctor-client relationship is important, because as vaccination guidelines change, there may not be an annual "vaccine visit" scheduled. You must make sure that you see your veterinarian at least annually, even if no vaccines are due, because this is the best opportunity to coordinate healthcare activities and to make sure that no medical issues creep by unaddressed.

When your American Bulldog reaches three-quarters of his anticipated lifespan, he is considered a "senior" and will require more attention to his health. In general, if you've been taking great care of your canine companion throughout his formative and adult years, the transition to senior status should be a smooth one. Age is not a disease, and as long as everything is functioning as it should, there is no reason why most of late adulthood should not be rewarding for both you and your pet. This is especially true if you have tended to the details, such as regular veterinary visits, proper dental care, excellent nutrition and management of bone and joint issues.

At this stage in your American Bulldog's life, your veterinarian may want to schedule visits twice yearly, instead of once, to run some laboratory screenings,

TAKING YOUR DOG'S TEMPERATURE

It is important to know how to take your dog's temperature at times when you think he may be ill. It's not the most enjoyable task, but it can be done without too much difficulty. It's easier with a helper, preferably someone with whom the dog is friendly, so that one of you can hold the dog while the other inserts the thermometer.

Before inserting the thermometer, coat the end with petroleum jelly. Insert the thermometer slowly and gently into the dog's rectum about one inch. Wait for the reading, about two minutes. Be sure to remove the thermometer carefully and clean it thoroughly after each use.

A dog's normal body temperature is between 100.5 and 102.5 degrees F. Immediate veterinary attention is required if the dog's temperature is below 99 or above 104 degrees F.

electrocardiograms and the like, and to change the diet to something more digestible. Catching problems early is the best way to manage them effectively. Treating the early stages of heart disease is so much easier than trying to intervene when there is more significant damage to the heart muscle. Similarly, managing the beginning of kidney problems is fairly routine if there is no significant kidney damage. Other problems, like cognitive dysfunction (similar to senility and Alzheimer's disease), cancer, diabetes and arthritis, are more common in older dogs, but all can be treated to help the dog live as many happy, comfortable years as possible. Just as in people, medical management is more effective (and less expensive) when you catch things early.

SELECTING A VETERINARIAN

There is probably no more important decision that you will make regarding your pet's healthcare than the selection of his doctor. Your pet's veterinarian will be a pediatrician, family-practice physician and gerontologist, depending on the dog's life stage, and will be the individual who makes recommendations regarding issues such as when specialists need to be consulted, when diagnostic testing and/or therapeutic intervention is needed and when you will need to seek outside emergency and critical-care services. Your vet will act as your advocate and liaison throughout these processes.

Everyone has his own idea about what to look for in a vet, an individual who will play a big role in his dog's (and, of course, his own) life for many years to come. For some, it is the compassionate caregiver with whom they hope to develop a professional relationship to span the lifetime of their dogs and even their future pets. For others, they are seeking a clinician with keen diagnostic and therapeutic insight who can deliver state-of-the-art healthcare. Still others need a veterinary facility that is open evenings and weekends, is in close proximity or provides mobile veterinary services to accommodate their schedules; these people may not much mind that their dogs might see different veterinarians on each visit. Just as we have different reasons for selecting our own healthcare professionals (e.g., covered by insurance plan, expert in field, convenient location), we should not expect that there is a one-size-fits-all recommendation for selecting a veterinarian and veterinary practice. The best advice is to be honest in your assessment of what you expect from a veterinary practice and to conscientiously research the options in your area. You will

What Is "Bloat" and How Do I Prevent it?

You likely have heard the term "bloat," which refers to gastric torsion (gastric dilatation/volvulus), a potentially fatal condition. It is directly related to feeding and exercise practices, and there is much that owners can do to reduce their dogs' risk. The term *dilatation* means that the dog's stomach is filled with air, while *volvulus* means that the stomach is twisted around on itself, blocking the entrance/exit points. Dilatation/volvulus is truly a deadly combination, although they also can occur independently of each other. An affected dog cannot digest food or pass gas, and blood cannot flow to the stomach, causing accumulation of toxins and gas along with great pain and rapidly occurring shock.

Many theories exist on what exactly causes bloat, but we do know that deep-chested breeds are more prone. Activities like eating a large meal, gulping water, strenuous exercise too close to mealtimes or a combination of these factors can contribute to bloat, though not every case is directly related to these more well-known causes. With that in mind, we can focus on incorporating simple daily preventives and knowing how to recognize the symptoms. In addition to the tips presented in this book, ask your vet about how to prevent and recognize bloat. An affected dog needs immediate veterinary attention, as death can result quickly. Signs include obvious restlessness/discomfort, crying in pain, drooling/excessive salivation, unproductive attempts to vomit or relieve himself, visibly bloated appearance and collapsing. Do not wait: get to the vet *right away* if you see any of these symptoms. The vet will confirm by x-ray if the stomach is bloated with air; if so, the dog must be treated *immediately*.

As varied as the causes of bloat are the tips for prevention, but some common preventive methods follow:

- Feed two or three small meals daily rather than one large one;
- Do not feed water before, after or with meals, but allow access to water at all other times;
- Never permit rapid eating or gulping of water;
- No exercise for the dog at least two hours before and (especially) after meals;
- Feed high-quality food with adequate protein, adequate fiber content and not too much fat and carbohydrate;
- Explore herbal additives, enzymes or gas-reduction products (only under a vet's advice) to encourage a "friendly" environment in the dog's digestive system;
- Avoid foods and ingredients known to produce gas;
- Avoid stressful situations for the dog, especially at mealtimes;
- Make dietary changes gradually, over a period of a few weeks;
- Do not feed dry food only;
- Although the role of genetics as a causative of bloat is not known, many breeders do not breed from previously affected dogs;
- Sometimes owners are advised to have gastroplexy (stomach stapling) performed on their dogs as a preventive measure.

Pay attention to your dog's behavior and any changes that could be symptomatic of bloat. Your dog's life depends on it!

YOUR DOG NEEDS TO VISIT THE VET IF:

- He has ingested a toxin such as antifreeze or a toxic plant; in these cases, administer first aid and call the vet right away
- His teeth are discolored, loose or missing or he has sores or other signs of infection or abnormality in the mouth
- He has been vomiting, has had diarrhea or has been constipated for over 24 hours; call immediately if you notice blood
- He has refused food for over 24 hours
- His eating habits, water intake or toilet habits have noticeably changed; if you have noticed weight gain or weight loss
- He shows symptoms of bloat, which requires *immediate* attention
- He is salivating excessively
- He has a lump in his throat
- He has a lump or bumps anywhere on the body
- He is very lethargic
- He appears to be in pain or otherwise has trouble chewing or swallowing
- His skin loses elasticity

Of course, there will be other instances in which a visit to the vet is necessary; these are just some of the signs that could be indicative of serious problems that need to be caught as early as possible.

quickly appreciate that not all veterinary practices are the same, and you will be happiest with one that truly meets your needs.

There is another point to be considered in the selection of veterinary services. Not that long ago, a single veterinarian would attempt to manage all medical and surgical issues as they arose. That was often problematic, because veterinarians are trained in many species and many diseases, and it was just impossible for general veterinary practitioners to be experts in every species, every breed, every field and every ailment. However, just as in the human healthcare fields, specialization has allowed general practitioners to concentrate on primary healthcare delivery, especially wellness and the prevention of infectious diseases, and to utilize a network of specialists to assist in the management of conditions that require specific expertise and experience. Thus there are now many types of veterinary specialists, including dermatologists, cardiologists, ophthalmologists, surgeons, internists, oncologists, neurologists, behaviorists, criticalists and others to help primary-care veterinarians deal with complicated medical challenges. In most cases, specialists see cases referred by primary-care veterinar-

ians, make diagnoses and set up management plans. From there, the animals' ongoing care is returned to their primary-care veterinarians. This important team approach to your pet's medical-care needs has provided opportunities for advanced care and an unparalleled level of quality to be delivered.

With all of the opportunities for your American Bulldog to receive high-quality veterinary medical care, there is another topic that needs to be addressed at the same time—cost. It's been said that you can have excellent healthcare or inexpensive health-care, but never both; this is as true in veterinary medicine as it is in human medicine. While veterinary costs are a fraction of what the same services cost in the human healthcare arena, it is still difficult to deal with unanticipated medical costs, especially since they can easily creep into hundreds or even thousands of dollars if specialists or emergency services become involved. However, there are ways of managing these risks. The easiest is to buy pet health insurance and realize that its foremost purpose is not to cover routine healthcare visits but rather to serve as an umbrella for those rainy days when your pet needs medical care and you don't want to worry about whether or not you can afford that care.

VACCINATIONS AND INFECTIOUS DISEASES

There has never been an easier time to prevent a variety of infectious diseases in your dog, but the advances we've made in veterinary medicine come with a price—choice. Now while choice concerning your dog's vaccinations is a good thing, it also has

PET INSURANCE

Pet insurance policies are very cost-effective (and very inexpensive by human health-insurance standards), but make sure that you buy the policy long before you intend to use it (preferably starting in puppyhood, because coverage will exclude pre-existing conditions) and that you are actually buying an indemnity insurance plan from an insurance company that is regulated by your state or province. Many insurance policy look-alikes are actually discount clubs that are redeemable only at specific locations and for specific services. An indemnity plan covers your pet at almost all veterinary, specialty and emergency practices and is an excellent way to manage your pet's ongoing healthcare needs.

Dogs that spend a lot of time playing and resting in the grass run the risk of picking up parasites or being bitten by insects. American Bulldogs can also be prone to skin allergies.

SIMULATED MEDICAL CONDITION FOR EDUCATIONAL PURPOSES ONLY.

Of unknown cause, acral lick disease is evidenced by a raw, open wound, usually on the dog's front leg.

never been more difficult for the pet owner (or the veterinarian) to make an informed decision about the best way to protect pets through vaccination.

Years ago, it was just accepted that puppies got a starter series of vaccinations and then annual "boosters" throughout their lives to keep them protected. As more and more vaccines became available, consumers wanted the convenience of having all of that protection in a single injection. The result was "multivalent" vaccines that crammed a lot of protection into a single syringe. The manufacturers' recommendations were to give the vaccines annually, and this was a simple enough protocol to follow. However, as veterinary medicine has become more sophisticated and we have started looking more at healthcare quandaries rather than convenience, it became necessary to reevaluate the situation and deal with some tough questions.

It is important to realize that whether or not to use a particular vaccine depends on the risk of contracting the disease against which it protects, the severity of the disease if it is contracted, the duration of immunity provided by the vaccine, the safety of the product and the needs of the individual animal. In a very general sense, rabies, distemper, hepatitis and parvovirus are considered core vaccine needs, while parainfluenza, *Bordetella bronchiseptica*, leptospirosis, coronavirus and borreliosis (Lyme disease) are considered non-core needs and best reserved for animals that demonstrate reasonable risk of contracting the diseases.

NEUTERING/SPAYING

Sterilization procedures (neutering for males/spaying for

HEREDITARY HEALTH

Fortunately, breeders report very few hereditary health problems in the American Bulldog. Probably the biggest health concerns in the breed are those that are directly related to the American Bulldog's natural strength and high activity level. Some examples include injuries to muscles and joints, broken bones, torn ligaments and broken teeth.

Common Infectious Diseases

Let's discuss some of the diseases that create the need for vaccination in the first place. Following are the major canine infectious diseases and a simple explanation of each.

Rabies: A devastating viral disease that can be fatal in dogs and people. In fact, vaccination of dogs and cats is an important public-health measure to create a resistant animal buffer population to protect people from contracting the disease. Vaccination schedules are determined on a government level and are not optional for pet owners; rabies vaccination is required by law in all 50 states.

Parvovirus: A severe, potentially life-threatening disease that is easily transmitted between dogs. There are four strains of the virus, but it is believed that there is significant "cross-protection" between strains that may be included in individual vaccines.

Distemper: A potentially severe and life-threatening disease with a relatively high risk of exposure, especially in certain regions. In very high-risk distemper environments, young pups may be vaccinated with human measles vaccine, a related virus that offers cross-protection when administered at four to ten weeks of age.

Hepatitis: Caused by canine adenovirus type 1 (CAV-1), but since vaccination with the causative virus has a higher rate of adverse effects, cross-protection is derived from the use of adenovirus type 2 (CAV-2), a cause of respiratory disease and one of the potential causes of canine cough. Vaccination with CAV-2 provides long-term immunity against hepatitis, but relatively less protection against respiratory infection.

Canine cough: Also called tracheobronchitis, actually a fairly complicated result of viral and bacterial offenders; therefore, even with vaccination, protection is incomplete. Wherever dogs congregate, canine cough will likely be spread among them. Intranasal vaccination with *Bordetella* and parainfluenza is the best safeguard, but the duration of immunity does not appear to be very long, typically a year at most. These are non-core vaccines, but vaccination is sometimes mandated by boarding kennels, obedience classes, dog shows and other places where dogs congregate to try to minimize spread of infection.

Leptospirosis: A potentially fatal disease that is more common in some geographic regions. It is capable of being spread to humans. The disease varies with the individual "serovar," or strain, of *Leptospira* involved. Since there does not appear to be much cross-protection between serovars, protection is only as good as the likelihood that the serovar in the vaccine is the same as the one in the pet's local environment. Problems with *Leptospira* vaccines are that protection does not last very long, side effects are not uncommon, and a large percentage of dogs (perhaps 30%) may not respond to vaccination.

Borrelia burgdorferi: The cause of Lyme disease, the risk of which varies with the geographic area in which the pet lives and travels. Lyme disease is spread by deer ticks in the eastern US and western black-legged ticks in the western part of the country, and the risk of exposure is high in some regions. Lameness, fever and inappetence are most commonly seen in affected dogs. The extent of protection from the vaccine has not been conclusively demonstrated.

Coronavirus: This disease has a high risk of exposure, especially in areas where dogs congregate, but it typically causes only mild to moderate digestive upset (diarrhea, vomiting, etc.). Vaccines are available, but the duration of protection is believed to be relatively short and the effectiveness of the vaccine in preventing infection is considered low.

There are many other vaccinations available, including those for *Giardia* and canine adenovirus-1. While there may be some specific indications for their use, and local risk factors to be considered, they are not widely recommended for most dogs.

PROBLEM: AND THAT STARTS WITH "P"

Urinary tract problems more commonly affect female dogs, especially those who have been spayed. The first sign that a urinary tract problem exists usually is a strong odor from the urine or an unusual color. Blood in the urine, known as hematuria, is another sign of an infection, related to cystitis, a bladder infection, bladder cancer or a blood-clotting disorder. Urinary tract problems can also be signaled by the dog's straining while urinating, experiencing pain during urination and genital discharge as well as excessive water intake and urination.

Excessive drinking, in and of itself, does not indicate a urinary tract problem. A dog who is drinking more than normal may have a kidney or liver problem, a hormonal disorder or diabetes mellitus. Behaviorists report a disorder known as psychogenic polydipsia, which manifests itself in excessive drinking and urination. If you notice your dog drinking much more than normal, take him to the vet.

females) are meant to accomplish several purposes. While the underlying premise is to address the risk of pet overpopulation, there are significant medical and behavioral benefits to the surgeries as well. For females, spaying prior to the first estrus (heat cycle) leads to a marked reduction in the risk of mammary cancer. There also will be no manifestations of "heat" to attract male dogs and no bleeding in the house. For males, there is prevention of testicular cancer and a reduction in the risk of prostate problems. In both sexes, there may be some limited reduction in aggressive behaviors toward other dogs, and some diminishing of urine marking, roaming and mounting.

While neutering and spaying do indeed prevent animals from contributing to pet overpopulation, even no-cost and low-cost neutering options have not eliminated the problem. Perhaps one of the main reasons for this is that individuals that intentionally breed their dogs and those that allow their animals to run at large are the main causes of unwanted offspring. Also, animals in shelters are often there because they were abandoned or relinquished, not because they came from unplanned matings. Neutering/spaying is important, but it should be considered in the context of the real causes of animals' ending up in shelters and eventually being euthanized.

One of the important considerations regarding neutering is that it is a surgical procedure. This sometimes gets lost in discussions of low-cost procedures and commoditization of the process. In females, spaying is specifically referred to as an ovariohysterectomy. In this procedure, a midline incision is made in the abdomen and the entire uterus and both ovaries are surgically removed. While this is a major invasive surgical procedure, it usually has few complications, because it is typically performed on healthy young animals. However, it is major surgery, as any woman who has had a hysterectomy will attest.

In males, neutering has traditionally referred to castration, which involves the surgical removal of both testicles. While still a significant piece of surgery, there is not the abdominal exposure that is required in the female surgery. In addition, there is now a chemical sterilization option, in which a solution is injected into each testicle, leading to atrophy of the sperm-producing cells. This can typically be done under sedation rather than full anesthesia. This is a relatively new approach, and there are no long-term clinical studies yet available.

Neutering/spaying is typically done around six months of age at most veterinary hospitals, although techniques have been pioneered to perform the procedures in animals as young as eight weeks of age. In general, the surgeries on the very young animals are done for the specific reason of sterilizing them before they go to their new homes. This is done in some shelter hospitals for assurance that the animals will definitely not produce any pups. Otherwise, these organizations need to rely on owners to comply with their wishes to have the animals "altered" at a later date, something that does not always happen.

THREADWORMS

Though less common than ascarids, hookworms and other nematodes, threadworms concern dog owners in the southwestern US and Gulf Coast area, where the climate is hot and humid. Living in the small intestine of the dog, this worm measures a mere 2 millimeters and is round. Like that of the whipworm, the threadworm's life cycle is very complex, and the eggs and larvae are passed through the feces. The cause of a deadly disease in humans, worms of the genus *Strongyloides* readily infect people; the handling of feces is the most common means of transmission. Threadworms are most often seen in young puppies; bloody diarrhea and pneumonia are symptoms. Sick puppies must be isolated and treated immediately; vets recommend a follow-up treatment one month later.

A scanning electron micrograph of a dog flea, *Ctenocephalides canis,* on dog hair.

EXTERNAL PARASITES

FLEAS

Fleas have been around for millions of years and, while we have better tools now for controlling them than at any time in the past, there still is little chance that they will end up on an endangered species list. Actually, they are very well adapted to living on our pets, and they continue to adapt as we make advances.

The female flea can consume 15 times her weight in blood during active reproduction and can lay as many as 40 eggs a day. These eggs are very resistant to the effects of insecticides. They hatch into larvae, which then mature and spin cocoons. The immature fleas reside in this pupal stage until the time is right for feeding. This pupal stage is also very resistant to the effects of insecticides, and pupae can last in the environment without feeding for many months. Newly emergent fleas are attracted to animals by the warmth of the animals' bodies, movement and exhaled carbon dioxide. However, when they first emerge from their cocoons, they orient towards light; thus when an animal passes between a flea and the light source, casting a shadow, the flea pounces and starts to feed. If the animal turns out to be a dog or cat, the reproductive cycle continues. If the flea lands on another type of animal, including a person, the flea will bite but will then look for a more appropriate host. An emerging adult flea can survive without feeding for up to 12 months but, once it tastes blood, it can survive off its host for only three to four days.

It was once thought that fleas spend most of their lives in the environment, but we now know that fleas won't willingly jump off a dog unless leaping to another dog or when physically removed by brushing, bathing or other manipulation. Flea eggs, on the other hand, are shiny and smooth, and they roll off the animal and into the environment. The eggs, larvae and pupae then exist in the environment, but once the adult finds a susceptible animal, it's home sweet home until the flea is forced to seek refuge elsewhere.

Since adult fleas live on the animal and immature forms survive in the environment, a successful treatment plan must address all stages of the flea life cycle. There are now several safe and effective flea-control products that can be applied on a monthly basis. These include fipronil, imidacloprid, selamectin and permethrin (found in several formulations). Most of these products have significant flea-killing rates within 24 hours. However, none of them will control the immature forms in the environment. To accomplish this, there are a variety of insect growth regulators that can be

FLEA PREVENTION FOR YOUR DOG

- Discuss with your veterinarian the safest product to protect your dog, likely in the form of a monthly tablet or a liquid preparation placed on the back of the dog's neck.
- For dogs suffering from flea-bite dermatitis, a shampoo or topical insecticide treatment is required.
- Your lawn and property should be sprayed with an insecticide designed to kill fleas and ticks that lurk outdoors.
- Using a flea comb, check the dog's coat regularly for any signs of parasites.
- Practice good housekeeping. Vacuum floors, carpets and furniture regularly, especially in the areas that the dog frequents, and wash the dog's bedding weekly.
- Follow up house-cleaning with carpet shampoos and sprays to rid the house of fleas at all stages of development. Insect growth regulators are the safest option.

THE FLEA'S LIFE CYCLE

What came first, the flea or the egg? This age-old mystery is more difficult to comprehend than the actual cycle of the flea. Fleas usually live only about four months. A female can lay 2,000 eggs in her lifetime.

Egg

Photo by Carolina Biological Supply Co.

After ten days of rolling around your carpet or under your furniture, the eggs hatch into larvae, which feed on various and sundry debris. In days or months, depending on the climate, the larvae spin cocoons and develop into the pupal or nymph stage, which quickly develop into fleas.

Larva

Photo by Carolina Biological Supply Co.

Pupa

These immature fleas must locate a host within 10 to 14 days or they will die. Only about 1% of the flea population exist as adult fleas, while the other 99% exist as eggs, larvae or pupae.

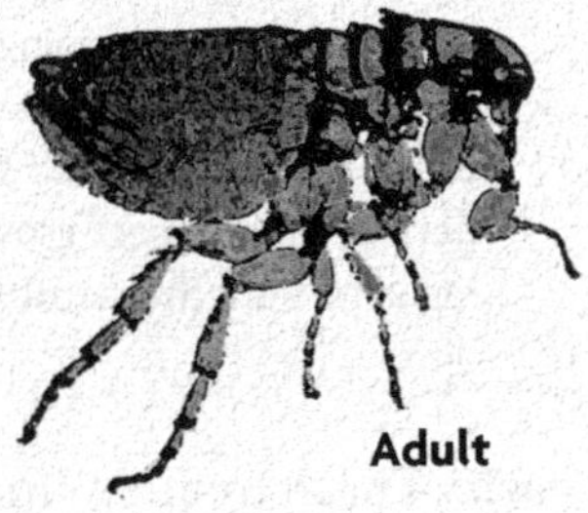

Adult

KILL FLEAS THE NATURAL WAY

If you choose not to go the route of conventional medication, there are some natural ways to ward off fleas:

- Dust your dog with a natural flea powder, composed of such herbal goodies as rosemary, wormwood, pennyroyal, citronella, rue, tobacco powder and eucalyptus.
- Apply diatomaceous earth, the fossilized remains of single-cell algae, to your carpets, furniture and pet's bedding. Even though it's not good for dogs, it's even worse for fleas, which will dry up swiftly and die.
- Brush your dog frequently, give him adequate exercise and let him fast occasionally. All of these activities strengthen the dog's system and make him more resistant to disease and parasites.
- Bathe your dog with a capful of pennyroyal or eucalyptus oil.
- Feed a natural diet, free of additives and preservatives. Add some fresh garlic and brewer's yeast to the dog's morning portion, as these items have flea-repelling properties.

sprayed into the environment (e.g., pyriproxyfen, methoprene, fenoxycarb) as well as insect development inhibitors such as lufenuron that can be administered. These compounds have no effect on adult fleas, but they stop immature forms from developing into adults. In years gone by, we relied heavily on toxic insecticides (such as organophosphates, organochlorines and carbamates) to manage the flea problem, but today's options are not only much safer to use on our pets but also safer for the environment.

TICKS

Ticks are members of the spider class (arachnids) and are bloodsucking parasites capable of transmitting a variety of diseases, including Lyme disease, ehrlichiosis, babesiosis and Rocky Mountain spotted fever. It's easy to see ticks on your own skin, but it is more of a challenge when your American Bulldog is affected. Whenever you happen to be planning a stroll in a tick-infested area (especially forests, grassy or wooded areas or parks) be prepared to do a thorough inspection of your dog afterward to search for ticks. Ticks can be tricky, so make sure you spend time looking in the ears, between the toes and everywhere else where a tick might hide. Ticks need to be attached for 24–72 hours before they transmit most of the diseases that they carry, so you do have a window of opportunity for some preventive intervention.

A TICKING BOMB

There is nothing good about a tick's harpooning his nose into your dog's skin. Among the diseases caused by ticks are Rocky Mountain spotted fever, canine ehrlichiosis, canine babesiosis, canine hepatozoonosis and Lyme disease. If a dog is allergic to the saliva of a female wood tick, he can develop tick paralysis.

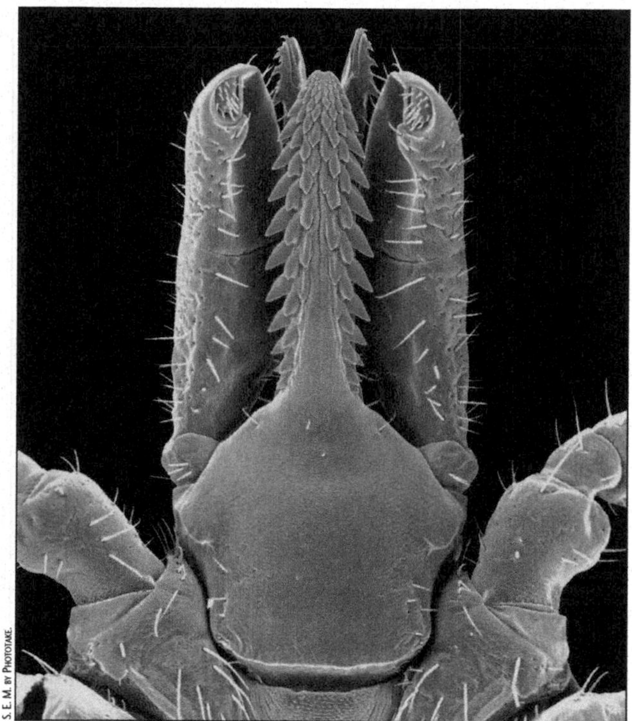

S.E.M. BY PHOTOTAKE.

A scanning electron micrograph of the head of a female deer tick, *Ixodes dammini*, a parasitic tick that carries Lyme disease.

Female ticks live to eat and breed. They can lay between 4,000 and 5,000 eggs and they die soon after. Males, on the other hand, live only to mate with the females and continue the process as long as they are able. Most ticks live on multiple hosts before parasitizing dogs. The immature forms typically reside on grass and shrubs, waiting for susceptible animals to walk by. The larvae and nymph stages typically feed on wildlife.

If only a few ticks are present on a dog, they can be plucked out, but it is important to remove the entire head and mouthparts,

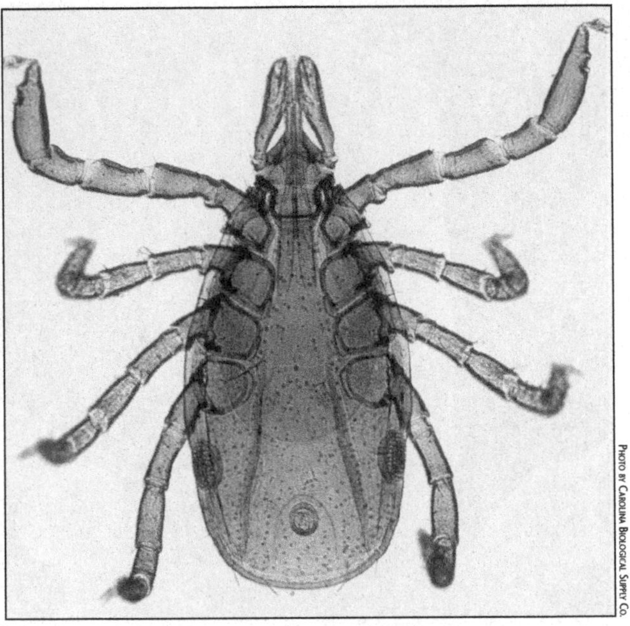
Photo by Carolina Biological Supply Co.

Deer tick, *Ixodes dammini.*

which may be deeply embedded in the skin. This is best accomplished with forceps designed especially for this purpose; fingers can be used but should be protected with rubber gloves, plastic wrap or at least a paper towel. The tick should be grasped as closely as possible to the animal's skin and should be pulled upward with steady, even pressure. Do not squeeze, crush or puncture the body of the tick or you risk exposure to any disease carried by that tick. Once the ticks have been removed, the sites of attachment should be disinfected. Your hands should then be washed with soap and water to further minimize risk of contagion. The tick should be disposed of in a container of alcohol or household bleach.

Some of the newer flea products, specifically those with fipronil, selamectin and permethrin, have effect against some, but not all, species of tick. Flea collars containing appropriate pesticides (e.g., propoxur, chlorfenvinphos) can aid in tick control. In most areas, such collars should be placed on animals in March, at the beginning of the tick season, and changed regularly. Leaving the collar on when the pesticide level is waning invites the development of resistance. Amitraz collars are also good for tick control, and the active ingredient does not interfere with other flea-control products. The ingredient helps prevent the attachment of ticks to the skin and will cause those ticks already on the skin to detach themselves.

TICK CONTROL

Removal of underbrush and leaf litter and the thinning of trees in areas where tick control is desired are recommended. These actions remove the cover and food sources for small animals that serve as hosts for ticks. With continued mowing of grasses in these areas, the probability of ticks' surviving is further reduced. A variety of insecticide ingredients (e.g., resmethrin, carbaryl, permethrin, chlorpyrifos, dioxathion and allethrin) are registered for tick control around the home.

Mites

Mites are tiny arachnid parasites that parasitize the skin of dogs. Skin diseases caused by mites are referred to as "mange," and there are many different forms seen in dogs. These forms are very different from one another, each one warranting an individual description.

Sarcoptic mange, or scabies, is one of the itchiest conditions that affects dogs. The microscopic *Sarcoptes* mites burrow into the superficial layers of the skin and can drive dogs crazy with itchiness. They are also communicable to people, although they can't complete their reproductive cycle on people. In addition to being tiny, the mites also are often difficult to find when trying to make a diagnosis. Skin scrapings from multiple areas are examined microscopically but, even then, sometimes the mites cannot be found.

Fortunately, scabies is relatively easy to treat, and there are a variety of products that will successfully kill the mites. Since the mites can't live in the environment for very long without feeding, a complete cure is usually possible within four to eight weeks.

Cheyletiellosis is caused by a relatively large mite, which sometimes can be seen even without a microscope. Often referred to as "walking dandruff," this also causes itching, but not usually as profound as with scabies.

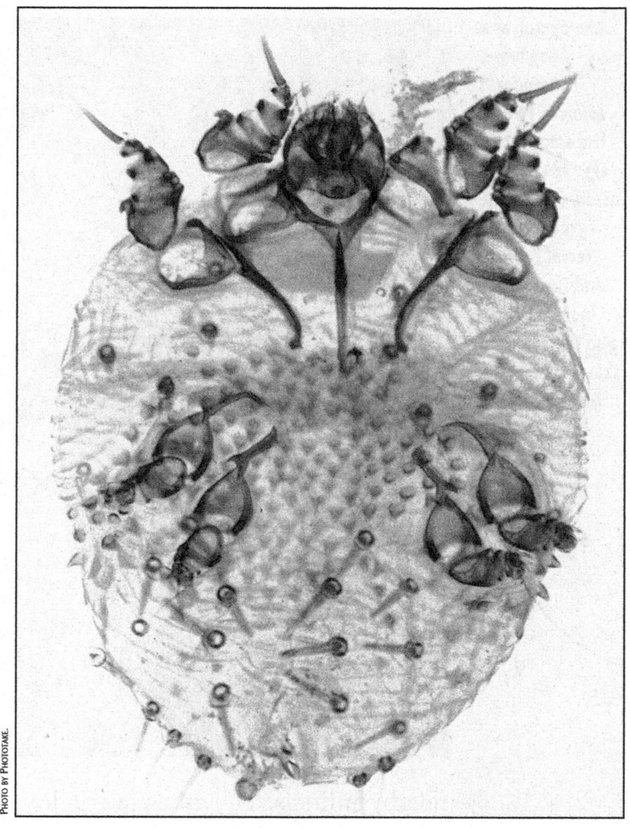

Photo by Phototake.

***Sarcoptes scabiei*, commonly known as the "itch mite."**

While *Cheyletiella* mites can survive somewhat longer in the environment than scabies mites, they too are relatively easy to treat, being responsive to not only the medications used to treat scabies but also often to flea-control products.

Otodectes cynotis is the canine ear mite and is one of the more common causes of mange, especially in young dogs in shelters or pet stores. That's because the mites are typically present in large numbers and are quickly spread to

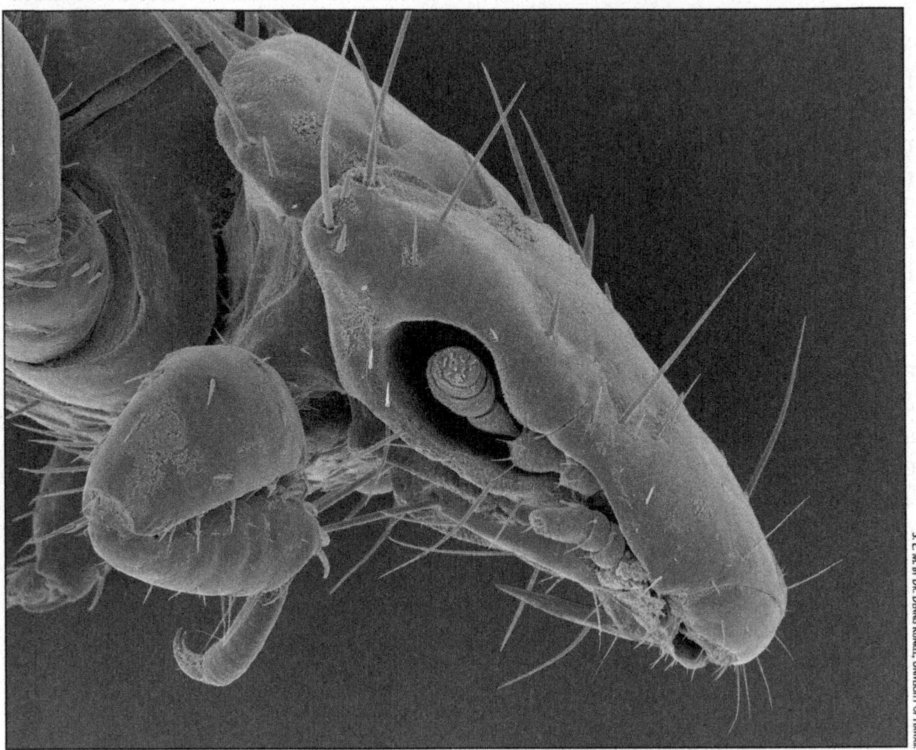

Micrograph of a dog louse, *Heterodoxus spiniger*. Female lice attach their eggs to the hairs of the dog. As the eggs hatch, the larval lice bite and feed on the blood. Lice can also feed on dead skin and hair. This feeding activity can cause hair loss and skin problems.

S.E.M. by Dr. Dennis Kunkel, University of Hawaii

nearby animals. The mites rarely do much harm but can be difficult to eradicate if the treatment regimen is not comprehensive. While many try to treat the condition with ear drops only, this is the most common cause of treatment failure. Ear drops cause the mites to simply move out of the ears and as far away as possible (usually to the base of the tail) until the insecticide levels in the ears drop to an acceptable level—then it's back to business as usual! The successful treatment of ear mites requires treating all animals in the household with a systemic insecticide, such as selamectin, or a combination of miticidal ear drops combined with whole-body flea-control preparations.

Demodicosis, sometimes referred to as red mange, is sometimes a problem in the American Bulldog and can be one of the most difficult forms of mange to treat. Part of the problem has to do with the fact that the mites live in the hair follicles and they are relatively well shielded from topical and systemic products. The main issue, however, is that demodectic mange typically results only when there is some underlying process interfering with the dog's immune system.

Since *Demodex* mites are normal residents of the skin of mammals, including humans, there is usually a mite population explosion only when the immune system fails to keep the number of mites in check. In young animals, the immune deficit may be transient or may reflect an actual inherited immune problem. In older animals, demodicosis is usually seen only when there is another disease hampering the immune system, such as diabetes, cancer, thyroid problems or the use of immune-suppressing drugs. Accordingly, treatment involves not only trying to kill the mange mites but also discerning what is interfering with immune function and correcting it if possible.

ILLUSTRATION BY PHOTOTAKE

Illustration of *Demodex folliculoram.*

Chiggers represent several different species of mite that don't parasitize dogs specifically, but do latch on to passersby and can cause irritation. The problem is most prevalent in wooded areas in the late summer and fall. Treatment is not difficult, as the mites do not complete their life cycle on dogs and are susceptible to a variety of miticidal products.

Mosquitoes

Mosquitoes have long been known to transmit a variety of diseases to people, as well as just being biting pests during warm weather. They also pose a real risk to pets. Not only do they carry deadly heartworms but recently there also has been much concern over their involvement with West Nile virus. While we can avoid heartworm with the use of preventive medications, there are no such preventives for West Nile virus. The only method of prevention in endemic areas is active mosquito control. Fortunately, most dogs that have been exposed to the virus only developed flu-like symptoms and, to date, there have not been the large number of reported deaths in canines as seen in some other species.

MOSQUITO REPELLENT

Low concentrations of DEET (less than 10%), found in many human mosquito repellents, have been safely used in dogs but, in these concentrations, probably give only about two hours of protection. DEET may be safe in these small concentrations, but since it is not licensed for use on dogs, there is no research proving its safety for dogs. Products containing permethrin give the longest-lasting protection, perhaps two to four weeks. As DEET is not licensed for use on dogs, and both DEET and permethrin can be quite toxic to cats, appropriate care should be exercised. Other products, such as those containing oil of citronella, also have some mosquito-repellent activity, but typically have a relatively short duration of action.

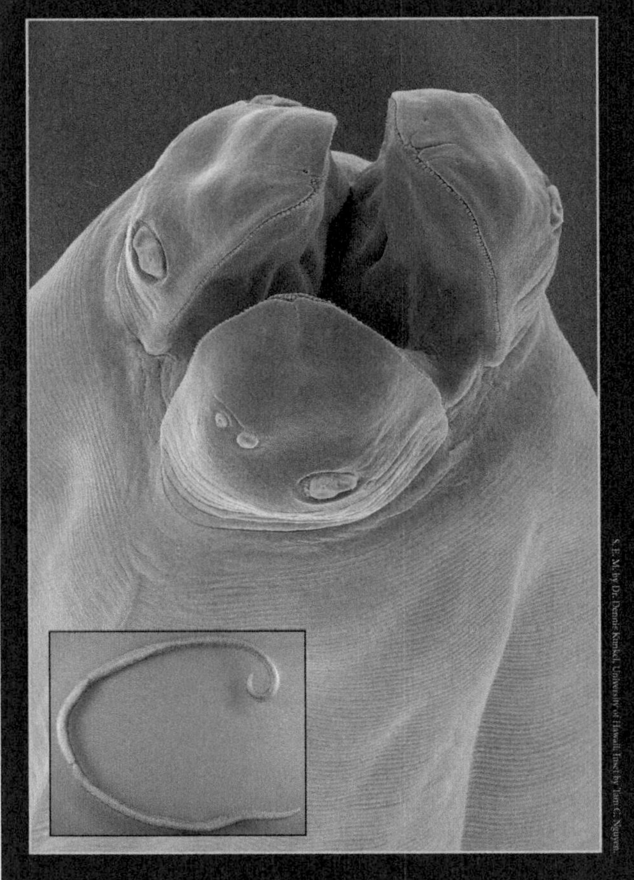

ASCARID DANGERS

The most commonly encountered worms in dogs are roundworms known as ascarids. *Toxascaris leonine* and Toxocara canis are the two species that infect dogs. Subsisting in the dog's stomach and intestines, adult roundworms can grow to 7 inches in length and adult females can lay in excess of 200,000 eggs in a single day.

In humans, visceral larval migrans affects people who have ingested eggs of Toxocara canis, which frequently contaminates children's sandboxes, beaches and park grounds. The roundworms reside in the human's stomach and intestines, as they would in a dog's, but do not mature. Instead, they find their way to the liver, lungs and skin, or even to the heart or kidneys in severe cases. Deworming puppies is critical in preventing the infection in humans, and young children should never handle nursing pups who have not been dewormed.

The ascarid roundworm *Toxocara canis,* showing the mouth with three lips. INSET: Photomicrograph of the roundworm *Ascaris lumbricoides.*

INTERNAL PARASITES: WORMS

Ascarids

Ascarids are intestinal roundworms that rarely cause severe disease in dogs. Nonetheless, they are of major public health significance because they can be transferred to people. Sadly, it is children who are most commonly affected by the parasite, probably from inadvertently ingesting ascarid-contaminated soil. In fact, many yards and children's sandboxes contain appreciable numbers of ascarid eggs. So, while ascarids don't bite dogs or latch onto their intestines to suck blood, they do cause some nasty medical conditions in children and are best eradicated from our furry friends. Because pups can start passing ascarid eggs by three weeks of age, most parasite-control programs begin at two weeks of age and are repeated every two weeks until pups are eight weeks old. It is important to

HOOKED ON *ANCYLOSTOMA*

Adult dogs can become infected by the bloodsucking nematodes we commonly call hookworms via ingesting larvae from the ground or via the larvae penetrating the dog's skin. It is not uncommon for infected dogs to show no symptoms of hookworm infestation. Sometimes symptoms occur within ten days of exposure. These symptoms can include bloody diarrhea, anemia, loss of weight and general weakness. Dogs pass the hookworm eggs in their stools, which serves as the vet's method of identifying the infestation. The hookworm larvae can encyst themselves in the dog's tissues and be released when the dog is experiencing stress.

Caused by an Ancylostoma species whose common host is the dog, cutaneous larval migrans affects humans, causing itching and lumps and streaks beneath the surface of the skin.

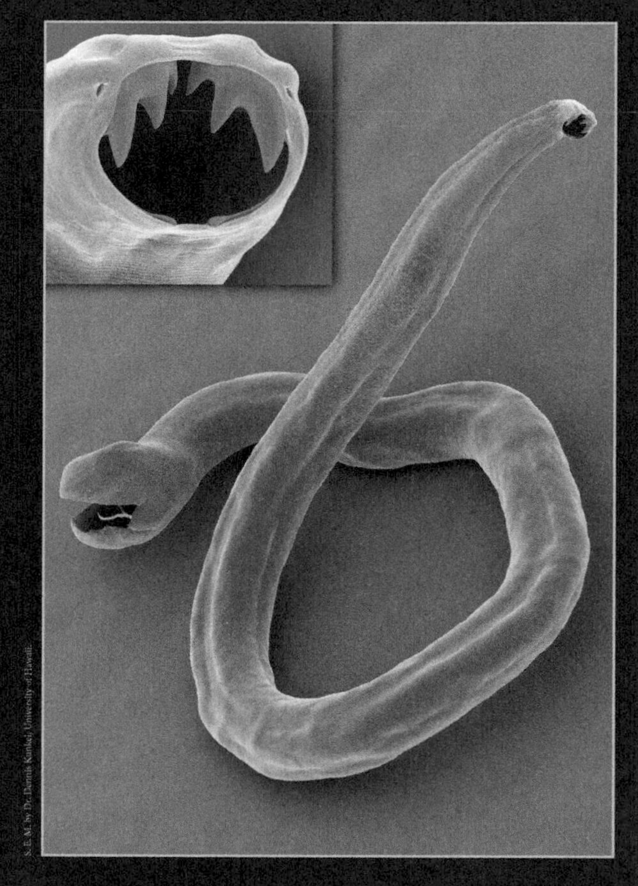

S.E.M. by Dr. Dennis Kunkel, University of Hawaii

The hookworm *Ancylostoma caninum* infests the intestines of dogs. INSET: Note the row of hooks at the posterior end, used to anchor the worm to the intestinal wall.

realize that bitches can pass ascarids to their pups even if they test negative prior to whelping. Accordingly, bitches are best treated at the same time as the pups.

Hookworms

Unlike ascarids, hookworms do latch onto a dog's intestinal tract and can cause significant loss of blood and protein. Similar to ascarids, hookworms can be transmitted to humans, where they cause a condition known as cutaneous larval migrans. Dogs can become infected either by consuming the infective larvae or by the larvae's penetrating the skin directly. People most often get infected when they are lying on the ground (such as on a beach) and the larvae penetrate the skin. Yes, the larvae can penetrate through a beach blanket. Hookworms are typically susceptible to the same medications used to treat ascarids.

WHIPWORMS

Whipworms latch onto the lower aspects of the dog's colon and can cause cramping and diarrhea. Eggs do not start to appear in the dog's feces until about three months after the dog was infected. This worm has a peculiar life cycle, which makes it more difficult to control than ascarids or hookworms. The good thing is that whipworms rarely are transferred to people.

Some of the medications used to treat ascarids and hookworms are also effective against whipworms, but, in general, a separate treatment protocol is needed. Since most of the medications are effective against the adults but not the eggs or larvae, treatment is typically repeated in three weeks, and then often in three months as well. Unfortunately, since dogs don't develop resistance to whipworms, it is difficult to prevent them from getting reinfected if they visit soil contaminated with whipworm eggs.

Adult whipworm, *Trichuris* sp., an intestinal parasite.

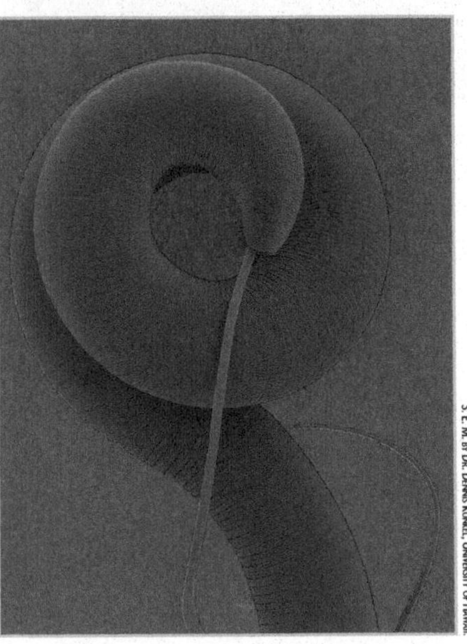

S. E. M. BY DR. DENNIS KUNKEL, UNIVERSITY OF HAWAII.

WORM-CONTROL GUIDELINES

- Practice sanitary habits with your dog and home.
- Clean up after your dog and don't let him sniff or eat other dogs' droppings.
- Control insects and fleas in the dog's environment. Fleas, lice, cockroaches, beetles, mice and rats can act as hosts for various worms.
- Prevent dogs from eating uncooked meat, raw poultry and dead animals.
- Keep dogs and children from playing in sand and soil.
- Kennel dogs on cement or gravel; avoid dirt runs.
- Administer heartworm preventives regularly.
- Have your vet examine your dog's stools at your annual visits.
- Select a boarding kennel carefully so as to avoid contamination from other dogs or an unsanitary environment.
- Prevent dogs from roaming. Obey local leash laws.

TAPEWORMS

There are many different species of tapeworm that affect dogs, but *Dipylidium caninum* is probably the most common and is spread by fleas. Flea larvae feed on organic debris and tapeworm eggs in the environment and, when a dog chews at himself and manages to ingest fleas, he might get a dose of tapeworm at the same time. The tapeworm then develops further in the intestine of the dog.

The tapeworm itself, which is a parasitic flatworm that latches onto the intestinal wall, is composed of numerous segments. When the segments break off into the intestine (as proglottids), they may accumulate around the rectum, like grains of rice. While this tapeworm is disgusting in its behavior, it is not directly communicable to humans (although humans can also get infected by swallowing fleas).

S. E. M. by Dr. Dennis Kunkel, University of Hawaii.

A dog tapeworm proglottid (body segment).

A much more dangerous flatworm is *Echinococcus multilocularis*, which is typically found in foxes, coyotes and wolves. The eggs are passed in the feces and infect rodents, and, when dogs eat the rodents, the dogs can be infected by thousands of adult tapeworms. While the parasites don't cause many problems in dogs, this is considered the most lethal worm infection that people can get. Take appropriate precautions if you live in an area in which these tapeworms are found. Do not use mulch that may contain feces of dogs, cats or wildlife, and discourage your pets from hunting wildlife. Treat these tapeworm infections aggressively in pets, because if humans get infected, approximately half die.

Heartworms

Heartworm disease is caused by the parasite *Dirofilaria immitis* and is seen in dogs around the world. A member of the roundworm group, it is spread between dogs by the bite of an infected mosquito. The mosquito injects infective larvae into the dog's skin with its bite, and these larvae develop under the skin for a period of time before making their way to the heart. There they develop into adults, which grow and create blockages of the heart, lungs and major blood vessels there. They also start producing offspring (microfilariae)

S. E. M. by Dr. Dennis Kunkel, University of Hawaii.

The dog tapeworm *Taenia pisiformis.*

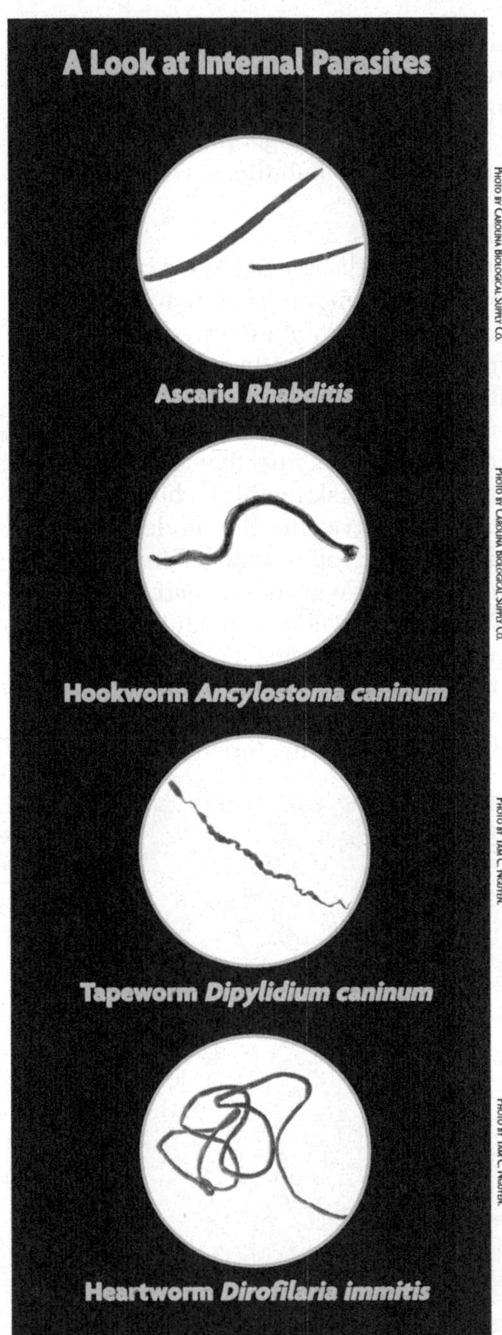

Ascarid *Rhabditis*

Hookworm *Ancylostoma caninum*

Tapeworm *Dipylidium caninum*

Heartworm *Dirofilaria immitis*

and these microfilariae circulate in the bloodstream, waiting to hitch a ride when the next mosquito bites. Once in the mosquito, the microfilariae develop into infective larvae and the entire process is repeated.

When dogs get infected with heartworm, over time they tend to develop symptoms associated with heart disease, such as coughing, exercise intolerance and potentially many other manifestations. Diagnosis is confirmed by either seeing the microfilariae themselves in blood samples or using immunologic tests (antigen testing) to identify the presence of adult heartworms. Since antigen tests measure the presence of adult heartworms and microfilarial tests measure offspring produced by adults, neither is positive until six to seven months after the initial infection. However, the beginning of damage can occur by fifth-stage larvae as early as three months after infection. Thus it is possible for dogs to be harboring problem-causing larvae for up to three months before either type of test would identify an infection.

The good news is that there are great protocols available for preventing heartworm in dogs. Testing is critical in the process, and it is important to understand the benefits as well as the limitations of such testing. All dogs six months of age or older that have not been on continuous heartworm-preventive medication should be

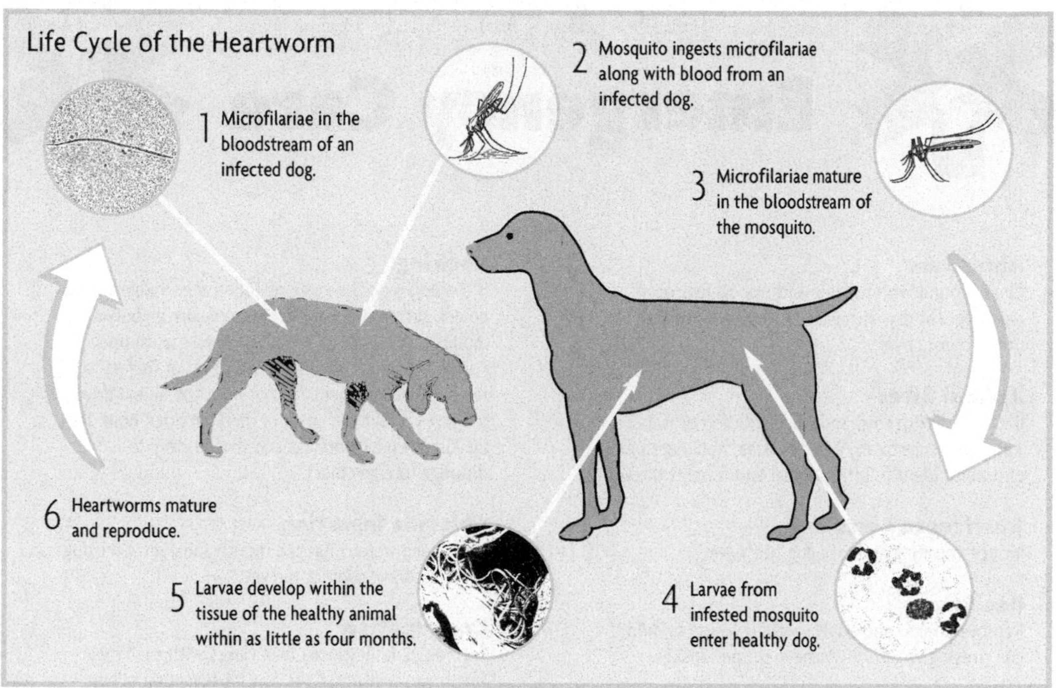

screened with microfilarial or antigen tests. For dogs receiving preventive medication, periodic antigen testing helps assess the effectiveness of the preventives. The American Heartworm Society guidelines suggest that annual retesting may not be necessary when owners have absolutely provided continuous heartworm prevention. Retesting on a two- to three-year interval may be sufficient in these cases. However, your veterinarian will likely have specific guidelines under which heartworm preventives will be prescribed, and many prefer to err on the side of safety and retest annually.

It is indeed fortunate that heartworm is relatively easy to prevent, because treatments can be as life-threatening as the disease itself. Treatment requires a two-step process that kills the adult heartworms first and then the microfilariae. Prevention is obviously preferable; this involves a once-monthly oral or topical treatment. The most common oral preventives include ivermectin (not suitable for some breeds), moxidectin and milbemycin oxime; the once-a-month topical drug selamectin provides heartworm protection in addition to flea, some types of tick and other parasite controls.

THE ABCs OF Emergency Care

Abrasions
Clean wound with running water or 3% hydrogen peroxide. Pat dry with gauze and spray with antibiotic. Do not cover.

Animal Bites
Clean area with soap and saline solution or water. Apply pressure to any bleeding area. Apply antibiotic ointment. Identify biting animal and contact the vet.

Antifreeze Poisoning
Induce vomiting and take dog to the vet.

Bee Sting
Remove stinger and apply soothing lotion or cold compress; give antihistamine in proper dosage.

Bleeding
Apply pressure directly to wound with gauze or towel for five to ten minutes. If wound does not stop bleeding, wrap wound with gauze and adhesive tape.

Bloat/Gastric Torsion
Immediately take the dog to the vet or emergency clinic; phone from car. No time to waste.

Burns
Chemical: Bathe dog with water and pet shampoo. Rinse in saline solution. Apply antibiotic ointment.

Acid: Rinse with water. Apply one part baking soda, two parts water to affected area.

Alkali: Rinse with water. Apply one part vinegar, four parts water to affected area.

Electrical: Apply antibiotic ointment. Seek veterinary assistance immediately.

Choking
If the dog is on the verge of collapsing, wedge a solid object, such as the handle of a screwdriver, between molars on one side of mouth to keep mouth open. Pull tongue out. Use long-nosed pliers or fingers to remove foreign object. Do not push the object down the dog's throat. For small or medium dogs, hold dog upside down by hind legs and shake firmly to dislodge foreign object.

Chlorine Ingestion
With clean water, rinse the mouth and eyes. Give dog water to drink; contact the vet.

Constipation
Feed dog 2 tablespoons bran flakes with each meal. Encourage drinking water. Mix 1/4-teaspoon mineral oil in dog's food. Contact vet if persists longer than 24 hours.

Diarrhea
Withhold food for 12 to 24 hours. Feed dog anti-diarrheal with eyedropper. When feeding resumes, feed one part boiled hamburger, one part plain cooked rice, 1/4- to 3/4-cup four times daily. Contact vet if persists longer than 24 hours.

Dog Bite
Snip away hair around puncture wound; clean with 3% hydrogen peroxide; apply tincture of iodine. Identify biting dog and call the vet. If wound appears deep, take the dog to the vet.

Frostbite
Wrap the dog in a heavy blanket. Warm affected area with a warm bath for ten minutes. Red color to skin will return with circulation; if tissues are pale after 20 minutes, contact the vet.

Use a portable, durable container large enough to contain all items.

Heat Stroke
Submerge the dog (up to his muzzle) in cold water; if no response within ten minutes, contact the vet.

Hot Spots
Mix 2 packets Domeboro® with 2 cups water. Saturate cloth with mixture and apply to hot spots for 15–30 minutes. Apply antibiotic ointment. Repeat every six to eight hours.

Poisonous Plants
Wash affected area with soap and water. Cleanse with alcohol. For foxtail/grass, apply antibiotic ointment. Contact vet if plant was ingested.

Rat Poison Ingestion
Induce vomiting. Keep dog calm, maintain dog's normal body temperature (use blanket or heating pad). Get to the vet for antidote.

Shock
Keep the dog calm and warm; call for veterinary assistance.

Snake Bite
If possible, bandage the area and apply pressure. If the area is not conducive to bandaging, use ice to control bleeding. Get immediate help from the vet.

Tick Removal
Apply flea and tick spray directly on tick. Wait one minute. Using tweezers or wearing plastic gloves, grasp the tick's body firmly. Apply antibiotic ointment.

Vomiting
Restrict water intake; offer a few ice cubes. Withhold food for next meal. Contact vet if vomiting persists longer than 24 hours.

DOG OWNER'S FIRST-AID KIT

- ❑ Gauze bandages/swabs
- ❑ Adhesive and non-adhesive bandages
- ❑ Antibiotic powder
- ❑ Antiseptic wash
- ❑ Hydrogen peroxide 3%
- ❑ Antibiotic ointment
- ❑ Lubricating jelly
- ❑ Rectal thermometer
- ❑ Nylon muzzle
- ❑ Scissors and forceps
- ❑ Eyedropper
- ❑ Syringe
- ❑ Anti-bacterial/fungal solution
- ❑ Saline solution
- ❑ Antihistamine
- ❑ Cotton balls
- ❑ Nail clippers
- ❑ Screwdriver/pen knife
- ❑ Flashlight
- ❑ Emergency phone numbers

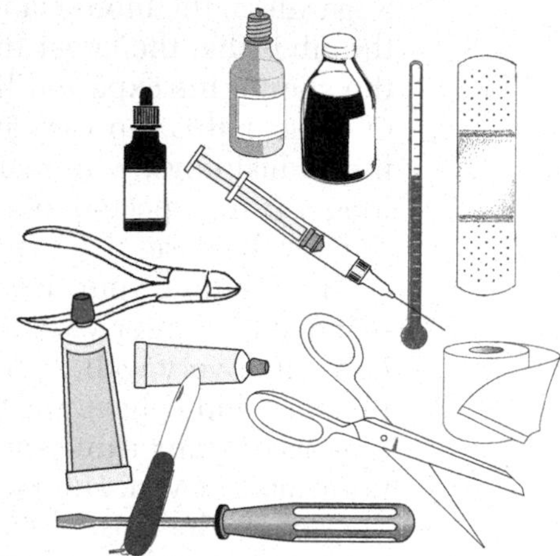

Your Senior

AMERICAN BULLDOG

As noted, pure-bred dogs are considered to have achieved senior status when they reach 75% of their breed's average lifespan, with lifespan being based on breed size. Your American Bulldog has an average lifespan of 10–12 years and thus is a senior citizen at around 7 or 8.

Obviously, the old "seven dog years to one human year" theory is not exact. In puppyhood, a dog's year is actually comparable to more than seven human years, considering the puppy's rapid growth during his first year. Then, in adulthood, the ratio decreases. Regardless, the more viable rule of thumb is that the larger the dog, the shorter his expected lifespan. Of course, this can vary among individual dogs, with many living longer than expected, which we hope is the case!

By the time your dog has reached his senior years, you will know him very well, so the physical and behavioral changes that accompany aging should be noticeable to you. Humans and dogs share the most obvious physical sign of aging: gray hair! Graying often occurs first on the muzzle and face, around the eyes. Other telltale signs are the dog's overall decrease in activity. Your older dog might be more content to nap and rest, and he may not show the same old enthusiasm when it's time to play in the yard or go for a walk. Other physical signs include significant weight loss or gain; more labored movement; skin and coat problems, possibly hair loss; sight and/or hearing problems; changes in toileting habits, perhaps seeming "unhousebroken" at times; tooth decay, bad breath or other mouth problems.

There are behavioral changes that go along with aging, too. There are numerous causes for behavioral changes. Sometimes a dog's apparent confusion results from a physical change like diminished sight or hearing. If his confusion causes him to be afraid, he may act aggressively or defensively. He may sleep more frequently because his daily walks, though shorter now, tire him out. He may begin to experience separation anxiety or, conversely, become less interested in petting and attention.

There also are clinical conditions that cause behavioral changes in older dogs. One such condition is known as canine cognitive dysfunction (familiarly known as "old-dog" syndrome). It can be frustrating for an owner whose dog is affected with cognitive dysfunction, as it can result in behavioral changes of all types, most seemingly unexplainable. Common changes include the dog's forgetting aspects of the daily routine, such as times to eat, go out for walks, relieve himself and the like. Along the same lines, you may take your dog out at the regular time for a potty trip and he may have no idea why he is there. Sometimes a placid dog will begin to show aggressive or possessive tendencies or, conversely, a hyperactive dog will start to "mellow out."

Disease also can be the cause of behavioral changes in senior dogs. Hormonal problems (Cushing's disease is common in older dogs), diabetes and thyroid disease can cause increased appetite, which can lead to aggression related to food guarding. It's better to be proactive with your senior dog, making more frequent trips to the vet if necessary and having bloodwork done to test for the diseases that can commonly befall older dogs.

The aforementioned changes are discussed to alert owners to the things that may happen as their dogs get older. Many hardy dogs remain active and alert well into old age. However, it can be frustrating and heartbreaking for owners to see their beloved dogs change physically and temperamentally. Just know that it's the same American Bulldog under there, and that he still loves you and appreciates your care, which he needs now more than ever.

Every dog is an individual in terms of aging. However, even if he shows no outward signs of

ADAPTING TO AGE

As dogs age and their once-keen senses begin to deteriorate, they can experience stress and confusion. However, dogs are very adaptable, and most can adjust to deficiencies in their sight and hearing. As these processes often deteriorate gradually, the dog makes adjustments gradually, too. Because dogs become so familiar with the layout of their homes and yards, and with their daily routines, they are able to get around even if they cannot see or hear as well. Help your senior dog by keeping things consistent around the house. Keep up with your regular times for walking and potty trips, and do not relocate his crate or rearrange the furniture. Your dog is a very adaptable creature and can make compensation for his diminished ability, but you want to help him along the way and not make changes that will cause him confusion.

aging, he should begin a senior-care program once he reaches the determined age. By providing him with extra attention to his veterinary care at this age, you will be practicing good preventive medicine, ensuring that the rest of your dog's life will be as long, active, happy and healthy as possible. If you do notice indications of aging, such as graying and/or changes in sleeping, eating or toileting habits, this is a sign to set up a senior-care visit with your vet right away to make sure that these changes are not related to any health problems.

To start, senior dogs should visit the vet twice yearly for exams, routine tests and overall evaluations. Many veterinarians have special screening programs especially for senior dogs that can include a thorough physical exam; blood test to determine complete blood count; serum biochemistry test, which screens for liver, kidney and blood problems as well as cancer; urinalysis; and dental exams. With these tests, it can be determined whether your dog has any health problems; the results also establish a baseline for your pet against which future test results can be compared.

In addition to these tests, your vet may suggest additional testing, including an EKG, tests for glaucoma and other problems of the eye, chest x-rays, screening for tumors, blood pressure test, test for thyroid function and screening for parasites and reassessment of his preventive program. Your vet also will ask you questions about your dog's diet and activity level, what you feed and the amounts that you feed. This information, along with his evaluation of the dog's overall condition, will enable him to suggest proper dietary changes, if needed.

Vets advise that older dogs need more frequent attention so that any health problems can be detected as early as possible. Serious conditions like kidney disease, heart disease and cancer may not present outward symptoms, or the problem may go undetected if the symptoms are mistaken by owners as just part of the aging process.

WEATHER WORRIES

Older pets are less tolerant of extremes in weather, both heat and cold. Your older dog should not spend extended periods in the sun; when outdoors in the warm weather, make sure he does not become overheated. In chilly weather, consider a sweater for your dog when outdoors and limit time spent outside. Whether or not his coat is thinning, he will need provisions to keep him warm when the weather is cold. You may even place his bed by a heating duct in your living room or bedroom.

Cognitive dysfunction shares much in common with senility and Alzheimer's disease. Dogs can become confused and/or disoriented, lose their house-training, have abnormal sleep-wake cycles and interact differently with their owners. There are many treatment options, though. There is good evidence that continued stimulation in the form of games, play, training and exercise can help to maintain cognitive function. There are also medications (such as seligiline) and antioxidant-fortified senior diets that have been shown to be beneficial.

Cancer is also a condition more common in the elderly. Almost all of the cancers seen in people are also seen in pets. If pets are getting regular physical examinations, cancers are often detected early. There are a variety of cancer therapies available today, and many pets continue to live happy lives with appropriate treatment.

Degenerative joint disease, often referred to as arthritis, is another malady common to both elderly dogs and humans. A lifetime of wear and tear on joints and running around at play eventually takes its toll and results in stiffness and difficulty in getting around. As dogs live longer and healthier lives, it is natural that they should eventually feel some of the effects of aging. If your pet was unfortunate enough to inherit hip dysplasia, osteochondritis dissecans or any of the other developmental orthopedic diseases, battling the onset of degenerative joint disease was probably a long-standing goal. In any case, there are now many effective remedies for managing degenerative joint disease and a number of remarkable surgeries as well.

There also is much you can do at home to keep your older dog in good condition. The dog's diet is an important factor. If your

RUBDOWN REMEDY

A good remedy for an aching dog is to give him a gentle massage each day, or even a few times a day if possible. This can be especially beneficial before your dog gets out of his bed in the morning. Just as in humans, massage can decrease pain in dogs, whether the dog is arthritic or just afflicted by the stiffness that accompanies old age. Gently massage his joints and limbs, as well as petting him on his entire body. This can help his circulation and flexibility and ease any joint or muscle aches. Massaging your dog has benefits for you, too; in fact, just petting our dogs can cause reduced levels of stress and lower our blood pressure. Massage and petting also help you find any previously undetected lumps, bumps or abnormalities. Often these are not visible and turn up only by being felt.

dog's appetite decreases, he will not be getting the nutrients he needs. He also will lose weight, which is unhealthy for a dog at a proper weight. Conversely, an older dog's metabolism is slower and he usually exercises less, but he should not be allowed to become obese. Obesity in an older dog is especially risky, because extra pounds mean extra stress on the body, increasing his vulnerability to heart disease. Additionally, the extra pounds make it harder for the dog to move about.

You should discuss age-related feeding changes with your vet. For a dog who has lost interest in food, it may be suggested that you try some different types of food until you find something new that the dog likes. For an obese dog, feeding a "light"-formula dog food or reducing food portions may be advised, along with providing exercise appropriate to his physical condition and energy level.

He may not be able to handle the morning run, long walks and vigorous games of fetch, but he still needs to get up and get moving. Keep up with your daily walks, but keep the distances shorter and let your dog set the pace. If he gets to the point where he's not up for walks, let him stroll around the yard. Base changes to the exercise program on your own individual dog and what he's capable of. Don't worry, your American Bulldog will let you know when it's time to rest.

Keep up with your grooming routine as you always have. Be extra-diligent about checking the skin and coat for problems. Older dogs can experience thinning coats as a normal aging process, but they can also lose hair as a result of medical problems. Some thinning is normal, but patches of baldness or the loss of significant amounts of hair is not.

Hopefully, you've been regular with brushing your dog's teeth throughout his life. Healthy teeth directly affect overall good health. We already know that bacteria from gum infections can enter the dog's body through the damaged gums and travel to the organs. At a stage in life when his organs don't function as well as they used to, you don't want anything to put additional strain on them. Clean teeth also contribute to a healthy immune system. Offering the dental-type chews in addition to toothbrushing can help, as they remove plaque and tartar as the dog chews.

Along with the same good care you've given him all of his life, pay a little extra attention to your dog in his senior years and keep up with twice-yearly trips to the veterinarian. The sooner a problem is uncovered, the greater the chances of a full recovery.

Number-One Killer Disease in Dogs: CANCER

In every age, there is a word associated with a disease or plague that causes humans to shudder. In the 21st century, that word is "cancer." Just as cancer is the leading cause of death in humans, it claims the lives of nearly half the dogs that die from a natural disease as well as half the dogs that die over the age of ten years.

Described as a genetic disease, cancer becomes a greater risk as the dog ages. Vets and dog owners have become increasingly aware of the threat of cancer to dogs. Statistics reveal that one dog in every five will develop cancer, the most common of which is skin cancer. Many cancers, including prostate, ovarian and breast cancers, can be avoided by spaying and neutering dogs by the age of six months.

Early detection of cancer can save or extend a dog's life, so it is absolutely vital for owners to have their dogs examined by a qualified vet or oncologist immediately upon detection of any abnormality. Certain dietary guidelines have also proven to deter the onset and spread of cancer. Foods based on fish rather than beef, due to the presence of omega-3 fatty acids, are recommended. Other amino acids such as glutamine have significant benefits for canines, particularly those breeds that show a greater susceptibility to cancer.

Cancer management and treatments promise hope for future generations of canines. Since the disease is genetic, breeders should never breed a dog whose parents, grandparents or any related siblings have developed cancer. It is difficult to know whether to exclude an otherwise healthy dog from a breeding program, as the disease does not manifest itself until the dog's senior years.

RECOGNIZE CANCER WARNING SIGNS

Since early detection can possibly rescue your dog from becoming a cancer statistic, it is essential for owners to recognize the possible signs and seek the assistance of a qualified professional.

- Abnormal bumps or lumps that continue to grow
- Bleeding or discharge from any body cavity
- Persistent stiffness or lameness
- Recurrent sores or sores that do not heal
- Inappetence
- Breathing difficulties
- Weight loss
- Bad breath or odors
- General malaise and fatigue
- Eating and swallowing problems
- Difficulty urinating and defecating

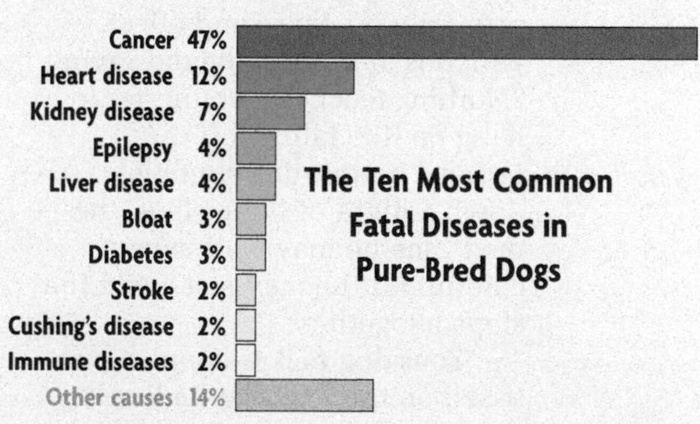

Behavior of Your
AMERICAN BULLDOG

You chose your dog because something clicked the minute you set eyes on him. Or perhaps it seemed that the dog selected you and that's what clinched the deal. Either way, you are now investing time and money in this dog, a true pal and an outstanding member of the family. Everything about him is perfect...well, almost perfect. Remember, he is a dog! For that matter, how does he think *you're* doing?

UNDERSTANDING THE CANINE MINDSET

For starters, you and your dog are on different wavelengths. Your dog is similar to a toddler in that both live in the present tense only. A dog's view of life is based primarily on cause and effect, which is similar to the old saying "Nothing teaches a youngster to hang on like falling off the swing." If your dog stumbles down a flight of three steps, the next time he may walk more carefully or he may just avoid the steps altogether.

Your dog makes connections based on the fact that he lives in the present, so when he is doing something and you interrupt to dispense praise or a correction, a connection, positive or negative, is made. To the dog, that's like one plus one equals two! In the same sense, it's also easy to see that when your timing is off, you will cause an incorrect connection. The one-plus-one way of thinking is why you must never scold a dog for behavior that took place an hour, 15 minutes or even 5 seconds ago. But it is also why, when your timing is perfect, you can teach him to do all kinds of wonderful things—as soon as he has made that essential connection. What helps the process is his desire to please you and to have your approval.

There are behaviors we admire in dogs, such as friendli-

PROFESSIONAL HELP

Every trainer and behaviorist asks, "Why didn't you come to me sooner?" Pet owners often don't want to admit that anything is wrong with their dogs. A dog's problem often is due to the dog and his owner mixing their messages, which will only get worse. Don't put it off; consult a professional to find out whether or not the problem is serious enough to require intervention.

ness and obedience, as well as those behaviors that cause problems to a varying degree. The dog owner who encounters minor behavioral problems is wise to solve them promptly or get professional help. Bad behaviors are not corrected by repeatedly shouting "No" or getting angry with the dog. Only the giving of praise and approval for good behavior lets your dog understand right from wrong. The longer a bad behavior is allowed to continue, the harder it is to overcome. A responsible breeder is often able to help. Each dog is unique, so try not to compare your dog's behavior with your neighbor's dog or the one you had as a child.

Have your veterinarian check the dog to see whether a behavior problem could have a physical cause. An earache or toothache, for example, could be the reason for a dog to snap at you if you were to touch his head when putting on his leash. A sharp correction from you would only increase the behavior. When a physical basis is eliminated, and if the problem is not something you understand or can cope with, ask for the name of a behavioral specialist, preferably one who is familiar with the American Bulldog. Be sure to keep the breeder informed of your progress.

Many things, such as environment and inherited traits, form the basic behavior of a dog, just as in humans. You also must factor into his temperament the purpose for which your dog was originally bred. The major obstacle lies in the dog's inability to explain his behavior to us in a way that we understand. The one thing you should not do is to give up and abandon your dog. Somewhere a misunderstanding has occurred but, with help and patient understanding on your part, you should be able to work out the majority of bothersome behaviors.

As an American Bulldog owner, you are responsible for keeping control of your large, powerful dog.

Those who know and love the American Bulldog usually get hooked on the breed.

AGGRESSION

"Aggression" is a word that is often misunderstood and is sometimes even used to describe what is actually normal canine behavior. For example, it's normal for puppies to growl when playing tug-of-war. It's puppy talk. There are different forms of dog aggression, but all are degrees of dominance, indicating that the dog, not his master, is (or thinks he is) in control. When the dog feels that he (or his control of the situation) is threatened, he will respond. The extent of the aggressive behavior varies with individual dogs. It is not at all pleasant to see bared teeth or to hear your dog growl or snarl, but these are signs of behavior that, if left uncorrected, can become extremely dangerous. A word of warning here: never challenge an aggressive dog. He is unpredictable and therefore unreliable to approach.

Nothing gets a "hello" from strangers on the street quicker than walking a puppy, but people should ask permission before petting your dog so you can tell the pup to sit in order to receive the admiring pats. If a hand comes down over the dog's head and he shrinks back, ask the person to bring their hand up, underneath the pup's chin. Now you're correcting strangers, too! But if you don't, it could make your dog afraid of strangers, which in turn can lead to fear-biting. Socialization prevents much aggression before it rears its ugly head.

The body language of an aggressive dog about to attack is clear. The dog will have a hard, steady stare. He will try to look as big as possible by standing stiff-legged, pushing out his chest, keeping his ears up and holding his tail up and steady. The hackles on his back will rise so that a ridge of hairs stands up. This posture may include the curled lip, snarl and/or growl, or he may be silent. He looks, and definitely is, very dangerous.

This dominant posture is seen

in dogs that are territorially aggressive. Deliverymen are constant victims of serious bites from such dogs. Territorial aggression is the reason you should never, *ever* try to train a puppy to be a watchdog. It can escalate into this type of behavior, over which you will have no control. All forms of aggression must be taken seriously and dealt with immediately. If signs of aggressive behavior continue, or grow worse, or if you are at all unsure about how to deal with your dog's behavior, get the help of a professional.

Uncontrolled aggression, sometimes called "irritable aggression," is not something for the pet owner to try to solve. If you cannot solve your dog's dangerous behavior with professional help, and you (quite rightly) do not wish to keep a canine time-bomb in your home, you will have some important decisions to make. Aggressive dogs often cannot be rehomed successfully, as they are dangerous and unreliable in their behavior. An aggressive dog should be dealt with only by someone who knows exactly the situation that he is getting into and has the experience, dedication and ideal living environment to attempt rehabilitating the dog, which often is not possible. In these cases, the dog ends up having to be humanely put down. Making a decision about euthanasia is not an easy undertaking for anyone, for any reason, but you cannot pass on to another home a dog that you know could cause harm.

Looks can be deceiving! A typical American Bulldog can seem intimidating, but those who know the breed will attest to its friendly and sometimes silly personality.

A milder form of aggression is the dog's guarding anything that he perceives to be his—his food dish, his toys, his bed and/or his crate. This can be prevented if you take firm control from the start. The young puppy can and should be taught that his leader will share but that certain rules apply. Guarding is mild aggression only in the beginning stages, and it will worsen and become dangerous if you let it.

Don't try to snatch anything away from your puppy. Bargain

for the item in question so that you can positively reinforce him when he gives it up. Punishment only results in worsening any aggressive behavior.

Many dogs extend their guarding impulse toward items they've stolen. The dog figures, "If I have it, it's mine!" (Some ill-behaved kids have similar tendencies.) An angry confrontation will only increase the dog's aggression. (Have you ever watched a child have a tantrum?) Try a simple distraction first, such as tossing a toy or picking up his leash for a walk. If that doesn't work, the best way to handle the situation is with basic obedience. Show the dog a treat, followed by calm, almost slow-motion commands: "Come. Sit. Drop it. Good dog," and then hand over the cheese! That's one example of positive-reinforcement training.

Children can be bitten when they try to retrieve a stolen shoe or toy, so they need to know how to handle the dog or to let an adult do it. They may also be bitten as they run away from a dog, in either fear or play. The dog sees the child's running as reason for pursuit, and even a

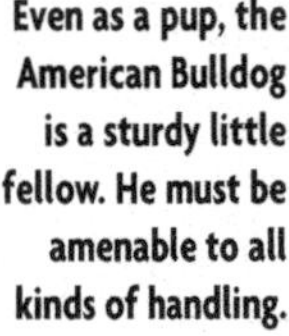

Even as a pup, the American Bulldog is a sturdy little fellow. He must be amenable to all kinds of handling.

friendly young puppy will nip at the heels of a runaway. Teach the kids not to run away from a strange dog and when to stop overly exciting play with their own puppy.

Fear biting is yet another aggressive behavior. A fear biter gives many warning signals. The dog leans away from the approaching person (sometimes hiding behind his owner) with his ears and tail down, but not in submission. He may even shiver. His hackles are raised, his lips curled. When the person steps into the dog's "flight zone" (a circle of 1 to 3 feet surrounding the dog), he attacks. Because of the fear factor, he performs a rapid attack-and-retreat. Because it is directed at a person, vets are often the victims of this form of aggression. It is frightening, but discovering and eliminating the cause of the fright will help overcome the dog's need to bite. Early socialization again plays a strong role in the prevention of this behavior. Again, if you can't cope with it, get the help of an expert.

Inter-Canine Aggression

Males are usually the ones given the "dog-aggressive" label, but both males and females can be aggressive toward dogs of their own sex, which is why good breeders will sometimes persuade the owner of a female to add a

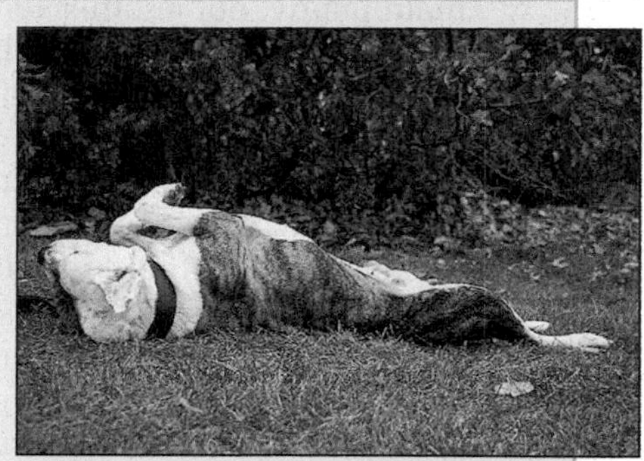

"DOG" SPOKEN HERE

Dogs' verbal language is limited to four words: growl, bark, whine and howl. Their body language is what tells the tale. They communicate with each other, and hopefully with you, through precise postures. You know what the friendly wagging tail and the play-bow (down in front, up in rear) mean, but there are many other things that you can decipher from your dog's body language. When the dog turns belly up, or on his side with one leg raised, he's being totally submissive. Looking away (breaking eye contact) and laid-back ears are other signs of submission. With ears at attention, mouth open and tail in a neutral position, the dog is watchful but relaxed. Fear is indicated by a crouching, even trembling, posture, with ears back, tail down and eyes averted. The aggressive dog attempts to look as large as possible to his adversary. He stalks stiffly, with his tail up, head high, ears alert, hackles raised, chest puffed out and lips curled, and with a stare that is cold and hard.

male puppy, not another female. Early spaying or neutering helps, but is not guaranteed to squelch all aggressive behavior.

Aggression is a dominant behavior, which is why you have repeatedly been told to socialize your puppy with other dogs as well as with people outside the family. Properly socialized dogs will greet each other in a friendly manner on the street or will live in harmony under one roof. Dogs that have not had the benefit of socialization experiences are ripe for becoming dog-aggressive.

Did you know that if you pull back on the leash as your dog meets another, you are signaling to your dog that you are afraid? The message goes right down the leash in a flash. His aggressive attitude in that case is your dog's way of protecting you. If you correct him for it, you'll have one very confused dog! If you are confronted with a dog that you consider or know to be aggressive, the best solution is to turn your dog's head away from the other dog (a head collar makes it easy to do) in order to break eye contact between the two. Then cross the street if you have to, crouch down to your dog's level and call him to you so you can praise him for a "good come."

If misfortune strikes and your dog gets into a true dogfight, stay out of it. Drop your dog's leash. Do not try to separate the dogs. Any intervention on your part will only exacerbate the aggression of both dogs, and you are sure to be bitten.

Dominant Aggression

In the wild, all canines operate on the pack system. Youngsters obey Mom and all older females, and all adult members of the pack obey the top male, who is the

Dogs smell each other as a means of getting acquainted.

leader of the pack. As young males mature, their allegiance shifts from Mom to the "boss man." Pups begin to learn the rules from the day their eyes and ears open, and they know that breaking the rules brings down the wrath of the pack kings and queens! They also know that there must always be just one leader, and each male has his eye on the position from adolescence.This Alpha system has been effective since the beginning for all pack animals. You can't change it, but you can make it work to your advantage.

Mounting is not always a sexual behavior; in some situations, it can be a display of dominance.

All of your training has to impress upon your puppy consistently that you are indeed the "top dog" in his pack. As he matures week after week, you will continue to reinforce that impression. Dogs are patiently cunning, and your dog will wait for the precise moment when you let down your guard and then *wham*! He will take over. If you let him, that is.

Keeping dominance under control is in your hands. Good-natured, gentle but firm, consistent training is the answer. Positive reinforcement will yield positive results. Correct poor or unwanted behavior by directing your dog into desirable behavior (via treats, distractions and obedience commands) and you will have turned a negative into a

CHASE INSTINCT

Chasing small animals is in the blood of many dogs, perhaps most; they think that this is a fun recreational activity (although some are more likely to bring you an undesirable "gift" as a result of the hunt). The good old "Leave it" command works to deter your dog from taking off in pursuit of "prey," but only if taught with the dog on leash for control.

Chasing cars or bikes is dangerous for all parties concerned: dogs, drivers and cyclists. Something about those wheels going around fascinates dogs, but that fascination can end in disastrous results. Corrections for your dog's chasing behavior must be immediate and firm. Tell him "Leave it!" and then give him either a sit or a down command. Get kids on bikes to help saturate your dog with spinning wheels while he politely practices his sits and stays.

At some dog shows, you must keep your dog in a crate while awaiting his turn in the ring. This requires a dog who is comfortable in a crate and won't mind the hustle and bustle of the crowds of dogs and people.

positive. Not too hard, but it takes patience to stay ahead of an exceptionally dominant dog. On the other hand, such a dog can be a lot of fun if you appreciate the challenge. Seeing through the ways in which he tries to outwit your leadership is thoroughly amusing. It would seem that dogs were the original "con artists." They will figure out how to trick you into doing what they want. How often do you fall for a sudden bark at the door, only to find that no one is there, and return to discover that the dog has taken your chair? Or how about when he asks to go out and instead leads you to the cookie jar? How many times has a throw toy been dropped expectantly in your lap? Dog language it may be, but it's pretty smart!

Veterinarians also suffer bites from dogs that are terrified of being put on the examination table. So putting your dog onto a grooming table (or a workbench or even a picnic table) for weekly grooming is another subtle way of telling him that you are in charge. At first the dog may find it a bit unsettling to be up off the ground on a small platform. However, once he knows he's safe and accepts that this is the place for his routine brushing, he won't have any fear or feelings of aggression when put onto the table at the veterinarian's.

SEPARATION ANXIETY

Any behaviorist will tell you that separation anxiety is the most common problem about which pet owners complain. It is also one of the easiest to prevent. Unfortunately, a behaviorist usually is not consulted until the

Praise and petting are a big part of forming a bond with your dog and rewarding him for appropriate behavior.

dog is a stressed-out, neurotic mess. At that stage, it is indeed a problem that requires the help of a professional.

Training the puppy to the fact that people in the house come and go is essential in order to avoid this anxiety. Leaving the puppy in his crate or a confined area while family members go in and out, and stay out for longer and longer periods of time, is the basic way to desensitize the pup to the family's frequent departures. If you are at home most of every day, make it a point to go out for at least an hour or two whenever possible.

How you leave is vital to the dog's reaction. Your dog is no fool. He knows the difference between sweats and business suits, jeans and dresses. He sees you pat your pocket to check for your wallet, open your briefcase, check that you have your cell phone or pick up the car keys. He knows from the hurry of the kids in the morning that they're off to school until afternoon. Lipstick? Aftershave lotion? Lunch boxes? Every move you make registers in his sensory perception and memory. Your puppy knows more about your departures than the FBI. You can't get away with a thing!

Before you got dressed, you checked the dog's water bowl and his supply of safe chew toys and you turned the radio on low. You

You want to be the one that your American Bulldog looks up to!

will leave him in what he considers his "safe" area, not with total freedom of the house. If you've invested in child safety gates, you can be reasonably sure that he'll remain in the designated area. Don't give him access to a window where he can watch you leave the house. If you're leaving for an hour or two, just put him into his crate with a safe toy.

Now comes the test! You are ready to walk out the door. Do not give your American Bulldog a big hug and a fond farewell. Do not drag out a long goodbye. Those are the very things that jump-start separation anxiety. Toss a biscuit into the dog's area, call out "So long, pooch" and close the door. You're gone. The chances are that the dog may bark a couple of times, or maybe whine once or twice, and then settle down to enjoy his biscuit and take a lovely nap, especially if you took him for a nice long walk before leaving. As he grows up, the barks and whines will stop because it's an old routine, so why should he make the effort?

When you first brought home the puppy, the come-and-go routine was intermittent and constant. He was put into his crate with a tiny treat. You left (silently) and returned in 3 minutes, then 5, then 10, then 15, then half an hour, until finally you could leave without a problem and be gone for 2 or 3 hours. If, at any time in the future, there's a "separation" problem, refresh his memory by going back to that basic training.

Now comes the next most important part—your return. Do not make a big production of coming home. "Hi, poochie" is as grand a greeting as he needs. When you've taken off your hat and coat, tossed your briefcase on the hall table and glanced at the mail, and the dog has settled down from the excitement of seeing you "in person" from his confined area, then go and give him a warm, friendly greeting. A potty trip is needed and a walk would be appreciated, since he's been such a good dog.

You want your American Bulldog to be well adjusted and confident, loving you and your family but feeling secure in your absence.

GET A WHIFF OF HIM!

Dogs sniff each other's rear as their way of saying "hi" as well as to find out who the other dog is and how he's doing. That's normal behavior between canines, but it can, annoyingly, extend to people. The command for all unwanted sniffing is "Leave it!" Give the command in a no-nonsense voice and move on.

DIGGING

Digging is another natural and normal doggie behavior. Wild canines dig to bury whatever food they can save for later to eat. (And you thought *we* invented the doggie bag!) Burying bones or toys is a primary cause to dig. Dogs also dig to get at interesting little underground creatures like moles and mice. In the summer, they dig to get down to cool earth. In winter, they dig to get beneath the cold surface to warmer earth.

The solution to the last two is easy. In the summer, provide a bed that's up off the ground and placed in a shaded area. In winter, the dog should either be indoors to sleep or given an adequate insulated doghouse outdoors. To understand how natural and normal this is, you have only to consider the Nordic breeds of sled dog who, at the end of the run, routinely dig a bed for themselves in the snow. It's the nesting instinct. How often have you seen your dog go round and round in circles, pawing at his blanket or bedding before flopping down to sleep?

Domesticated dogs also dig to escape, and that's a lot more dangerous than it is destructive. A dog that digs under the fence is the one that is hit by a car or becomes lost. A good fence to protect a digger should be set 12 inches below ground level, and every fence needs to be routinely checked for even the smallest openings that can become possible escape routes.

Catching your dog in the act of digging is the easiest way to stop it, because your dog will make the "one-plus-one" connection, but digging is too often a solitary occupation, something the lonely dog does out of boredom. Catch your young puppy in the act and put a stop to it before you have a yard full of craters. It is more difficult to stop if your dog sees you gardening. If you can dig, why can't he? Because you say so, that's why! Some dogs are excavation experts, and some dogs never dig. However, when it comes to any of these instinctive canine behaviors, never say "never."

THE MACHO DOG

The Venus/Mars differences are found in dogs, too. Males have distinct behaviors that, while seemingly sex-related, are more closely connected to the role of the male as leader. Marking territory by urinating on it is one means that male dogs use to establish their presence. Doing so merely says, "I've been here." Small dogs often attempt to lift their legs higher on the tree than the previous male. While this is natural behavior outdoors on items like telephone poles, fence posts, fire hydrants and most other upright objects, marking indoors is totally unacceptable. Treat it as you would a house-training accident and clean thoroughly to eradicate the scent. Another behavior often seen in the macho male, mounting is a dominance display. Neutering the dog before six months of age helps to deter this behavior. You can discourage him from mounting by catching the dog as he's about to mount you, stepping quickly aside and saying "Off!"

JUMPING UP

Jumping up is a device of enthusiastic, attention-seeking puppies, but adult dogs often like to jump up as well, usually as a form of canine greeting. This is a controversial issue. Some owners wouldn't have it any other way! They encourage their dogs, and the owners and dogs alike enjoy the friendly physical

"LEAVE IT"

Watch your puppy like a hawk to be certain it's a toy he's chewing, not your wallet. When you catch him in the act, tell him "Leave it!" and substitute a proper toy. Chewing on anything other than his own safe toys is countered by spraying the desirable (to the dog) object with a foul-tasting chew-deterrent product and being more diligent in your observations of his chewing habits. When you can't supervise, it's crate time for Fido.

contact. Some owners think that it's cute when it comes from a puppy, but not from an adult.

Conversely, there are those who consider jumping up to be one of the worst kinds of bad manners to be found in a dog. Among this group inevitably are bound to be some of your best friends. There are two situations in which your dog should be restrained from any and all jumping up. One is around children, especially young children and those who are not at ease with dogs. The other is when you are entertaining guests. No one who comes dressed up for a party wants to be groped by your dog, no matter how friendly his intentions or how clean his paws. The American Bulldog is a large dog, so you can't blame someone for being less then enthusiastic about that type of eager greeting.

The solution to this problem is relatively simple. If the dog has already started to jump up, the first command is "Off," followed immediately by "Sit." The dog must sit every time you are about to meet a friend on the street or when someone enters your home, be it child or adult. You may have to ask people to ignore the dog for a few minutes in order to let his urge for an enthusiastic greeting subside. If your dog is too exuberant and won't sit still, you'll have to work harder by first telling him "Off" and then issuing the down/stay command. This requires more work on your part, because the down is a submissive position and your dog is only trying to be super-friendly. A small treat is expected when training for this particular down.

If you have a real pet peeve about a dog's jumping up, then disallow it from the day your puppy comes home. Jumping up is a subliminally taught human-to-dog greeting. Dogs don't greet each other in this way. It begins because your puppy is close to the ground and he's easier to pet and cuddle if he reaches up and you bend over to meet him halfway. If you won't like it later, don't start it when he is young, but do give lots of praise and affection for a good sit.

BARKING

Here's a big, noisy problem! Telling a dog he must never bark is like telling a child not to speak! Consider how confusing it must be to your dog that you are using your voice (which is your form of barking) to teach him when to bark and when not to! That is precisely the reason not to "bark back" when the dog's barking is annoying you (or your neighbors). Try to understand the scenario from the dog's viewpoint. He barks. You bark. He barks again; you bark again. This "conversation" can go on forever!

The first time your adorable little puppy said "Yip" or "Yap, you were ecstatic. His first word! You smiled, you told him how smart he was—and you allowed him to do it. So there's that one-plus-one thing again, because he will understand by your happy reaction that "Mr. Alpha loves it when I talk." Ignore his barking in the beginning, and allow it, but don't encourage barking during play. Instead, use the "put a toy in it" method to tone it down. Add a very soft "Quiet" as you hand off the toy. If the barking continues, stand up straight, fold your arms and turn your back on the dog. If he barks, you won't play, and you should follow the same rule for all undesirable behavior during play.

Barking can be a dog's way of making his presence known to those on the other side of the fence.

> **DID YOU HEAR THAT?**
>
> Dogs can lead you to think that they are the best watchdogs in the world when they're only barking at falling leaves or twinkling stars! (In which case, you should bring them indoors!) Dogs bark when they have nothing else to do. (In which case, they need appropriate distractions.) They continue to bark if, when they did it the first time, you reacted as if you thought it was cute. (Don't encourage them!) Dogs bark as they sit in the window, watching the world go by. (Draw the blinds!) Your dog needs to learn that one bark is all it takes to alert you. That's enough.

Dogs bark in reaction to sounds and sights. Another dog's bark, a person passing by or even just rustling leaves can set off a barker. If someone coming up

PANHANDLING POOCHES

If there's one thing at which dogs excel, it is begging. If there's one thing that owners lack, it's the willpower to resist giving in to their canine beggars! If you don't give in to your adorable puppy, he won't grow into an adult dog that's a nuisance. However, give in just once and the dog will forever figure, "maybe this time." Treats are rewards for correct performance, a category into which begging definitely does not fall.

your driveway or to your door provokes a barking frenzy, use the saturation method to stop it. Have several friends come and go every three or four minutes over as long a period of time as they can spare (it could take a couple of hours). Attach about a foot of rope to the dog's collar and have very small treats handy. Each time a car pulls up or a person approaches, let the dog bark once (grab the rope if you need to physically restrain him), say "Okay, good dog," give him a treat and make him sit. "Okay" is the release command. It lets the dog know that he has alerted you and tells him that you are now in charge. That person leaves and the next arrives, and so on and so on until everyone—especially the dog—is bored and the barking has stopped. Don't forget to thank your friends. Your neighbors, by the way, may be more than willing to assist you in this parlor game if it means a quiet dog on the block.

We all love our dogs and our dogs love us. It may be hard to resist puckering up for a pooch smooch, but there are more sanitary ways to show affection to your pup.

Excessive barking outdoors is more difficult to keep in check, because when it happens, he is outside and you are probably inside. A few warning barks are fine, but use the same method to tell him when enough is enough. You will have to stay outside with him for that bit of training.

There is one more kind of vocalizing, which is called "idiot barking" (from idiopathic, meaning of unknown cause). It is usually rhythmic or a timed series of barks. Put a stop to it immediately by calling the dog to come. This form of barking can drive neighbors crazy and commonly occurs when a dog is left outside at night or for long periods of time during the day. He is completely and thoroughly bored! A change of scenery may help, such as relocating him to a room indoors when he is used to being outside.

A few new toys or different dog biscuits might be the solution. If he is left alone and no one can get home during the day, a noontime walk with a local dog-sitter would be the perfect solution.

EATING EXCREMENT

The unpleasant subject of dogs' eating their own feces, known as coprophagia, can be dealt with relatively easily even though no one is exactly sure why dogs do this. Some say it is primordial, while others feel that it indicates a lack of something in the diet (but there's no agreement as to what that "something" is). Unless the dog has worms, feces eating cannot make him sick, but that is no reason to allow it to continue. There are products said to alleviate the problem, but check with your vet before adding anything to your puppy's diet. Sprinkling hot pepper on the feces is an after-the-fact solution. Prevention (including keeping a clean yard) is the better way to go.

When you house-trained your dog, you took him outside on a leash and stayed with him until he did his business. Afterward, you moved him away or took him back indoors while you went back and cleaned up the feces. You were not giving him any opportunity to indulge in this strange canine habit. Now that your dog goes outside alone, watch to see that it doesn't start. At his first sign of interest in his own excrement, or that of any other animal, give him a sharp "No! Leave it!" and then bring the dog indoors so you can do your clean-up job. To clean up after your dog on the street, use a plastic bag over your hand to pick up the feces. In your yard, a "poop-scoop" is the easiest answer.

Cat feces entice many dogs, possibly because they have a different, often fishy, odor. If you have cats, look into buying one of the litter boxes that are made with narrow tunnel entrances to deter all but the most insistent of dogs. Keep the litter clean and the box in a spot that's inaccessible to your dog.

STOP, THIEF!

The easiest way to prevent a dog from stealing food is to stop this behavior before it starts by never leaving food out where he can reach it. However, if it is too late and your dog has already made a steal, you must stop your furry felon from becoming a repeat offender. Once Sneaky Pete has successfully stolen food, place a bit of food where he can reach it. Place an empty soda can with some pebbles in it on top of the food. Leave the room and watch what happens. As the dog grabs the tasty morsel, the can comes with it. The noise of the tumbling pebble-filled can makes its own correction, and you don't have to say a word.

Birth Date ______

Origin (Breeder's Name) ______

Breeder's Address ______

Breeder's Phone ______

Registration/ID Number ______

Distinguishing Features ______
IN CASE OF LOST DOG

Vet's Name ______

Vet's Address ______

Vet's Phone ______

VACCINATION RECORD					
VACCINE	DATES				

CPSIA information can be obtained
at www.ICGtesting.com
Printed in the USA
LVOW02s0046021216
515428LV00002B/11/P